THAT CALCUTTA . . .
THOSE BONGS!

THAT CALCUTTA . . .
THOSE BONGS!

Dipanwita Mukherjee

Rupa . Co

First Published 2010
Second Impression 2010

Published by

Rupa . Co

7/16, Ansari Road, Daryaganj
New Delhi 110 002

Sales Centres:

Allahabad Bengaluru Chandigarh Chennai
Hyderabad Jaipur Kathmandu
Kolkata Mumbai

Typeset by
Mindways Design
1410 Chiranjiv Tower
43 Nehru Place
New Delhi 110 019

Printed in India by
Nutech Photolithographers
B-240, Okhla Industrial Area, Phase-I,
New Delhi 110 020, India

In memory of those humble but brave people of my childhood who lived life with a gusto and passed on to me memorable lessons on how to transmute the ordinary into immortal.

Contents

Acknowledgements

I would like to thank my friends and family, whose faith in me gave me the courage to write this book.

Spring Onion Greens

'DON'T TOUCH THAT!'

The newly-married Bipasha jumped and dropped the *kadai* she had picked up. Hastily, she covered her head with her sari, which she had let fall below her shoulders as the kitchen was rather warm.

She turned to look blankly at her mother-in-law and thought fearfully, 'What have I done now?'

'I saw that you didn't wash your hands after cooking the fish!'

Her tone was accusing and Bipasha felt like a thief.

'Oh!' she replied, confused, trying to remember what she had done before picking up the kadai. No. She remembered now. She hadn't washed her hands.

'You know that I keep my utensils separate from the *amish* ones. Next time please remember to wash your hands before you touch my things.'

'Oh,' Bipasha said again, looking at her hands, as if they were to blame.

Quickly she went to the sink and opened the tap.

The old lady left, grumbling and Bipasha knew that a big issue would be made about this in the next room, where mother-in-law would be joined by her daughter.

Puti was half of Bipasha's age but always made her feel like a naughty schoolgirl, caught in the act. Frankly, she had never lived with a widow before and had no idea about these intimidating customs.

The first day she had been taken to the kitchen and given charge of the cooking, the arrangements had been explained. 'This side of the shelf,' Puti had said, pointing to the right of the gas stove, 'is the *niramish* side. And that,' pointing to the left, 'is amish.'

Right, vegetarian, left, non-vegetarian. She had noted it carefully, silently, though it had left her completely baffled. What's the point of all this?

'All the utensils on this side,' Puti continued, pointing to the right side of the lower shelf, 'are Ma's. All these on the left are ours.'

Then, as an afterthought, she had added, 'We keep a gap between the two lots. They are not supposed to touch each other.'

Later, she had shown her how everytime after they cooked a non-vegetarian item, everything was wiped with a wet rag, including the stove and the burners, before they cooked anything vegetarian. No wonder the burners were so rusted, she thought, but didn't dare to say anything. Puti had been in one of her rare good moods and Bipasha didn't want to spoil it. She was eager to build a good relationship with the family and if it meant taking over the cooking, she was ready to do it.

She realised soon enough that the job wasn't as easy as she thought it was going to be. Initially, she kept forgetting which side was vegetarian, and which side was non-vegetarian. Then, the hired help, who cleaned the utensils, often was in a big hurry and left the utensils too close to each other, so that a spatula or a ladle would roll into the other side and became indistinguishable.

'That's not Ma's spatula!'

'Oh, no, you've mixed up the ladle again!'

These were some of the comments she kept on hearing time and again.

'I'm doing my best,' she said in tears one day, to her husband, after she had been snapped at, by mother and daughter a bit too many times. 'I'm just not used to this system, you know.'

'For God's sake!' her husband had said in disgust, 'This is the 70s! Why can't she give up these stupid customs and adjust a bit?'

But Bipasha did not want to get into these petty little problems as she knew that ultimately, she was the one who would be blamed for drawing him into it. So she wiped her tears and pretended that it wasn't such an important issue. What could he do, anyway? Bengali sons don't take their wives' sides against their poor widowed mothers and fatherless sisters.

One was supposed to be mature enough to handle such issues by oneself.

At her mother's place, Bipasha's sisters stood wide-eyed in wonder as she described the kitchen arrangements at her in-law's place.

'But if she doesn't even *touch* anything amish, as you say, how come she touches the platform on which they are kept?' her younger sister asked.

'And not only that,' Bipasha continued warming up to their curiosity, 'she has *mushurir daal* in the morning. But come evening, it becomes untouchable!'

Bipasha's mother, though, knew about such customs.

'Rice, and anything prepared from rice cannot be eaten after sunset, as well,' she added, to the amazement of her daughters.

'Well, how was I to know,' Bipasha complained, 'You should have told me before.'

'In your grandmother's time, they followed these rules strictly. But in those days, they had separate vegetarian and non-vegetarian kitchens,' she replied. 'I never thought your mother-in-law was so old-fashioned.'

'Come to think of it, in that case, puffed rice and split rice should also be untouchable,' Bipasha pondered.

'Well, all these rules must have had their own logic,' her mother said, 'Don't worry, you'll get used to it in time.'

'So, you must have been in deep sea, Didi,' her younger sister asked, 'How did you manage?'

'Not well at all. I kept on making mistakes at first. But now, I think, I've got it under control.'

'Poor Didi.'

'I'll never marry into a traditional family,' the youngest sister declared. 'At least I'll make sure I don't have a mother-in-law. A widowed mother-in-law is absolute no-no,' she giggled.

'Shh. . . . !' the older one warned, 'Mother will kill you if she hears you say things like that.'

When she returned after her holiday, Bipasha was confident that she had learnt everything she had to know about her in-law's kitchen. One evening she rummaged in the crisper box, looking for something to cook for her mother-in-law's dinner. She usually had two chapattis with a vegetable curry. Bipasha found a bunch of spring onion greens. How about a potato-and-spring-onion curry? She had never cooked it before and thought that it would be a nice change. She was tired of the usual brinjals and cabbages and pumpkins and other insipid summer vegetables. Her mother used to make this curry really well and she tried remembering the recipe. Quietly, without consulting anyone, she took out the greens and decided to surprise the old lady. She peeled and cut the potatoes into thin strips and then chopped the greens neatly and finely. She hadn't noticed when her mother-in-law had crept up to the kitchen door. She always walked barefoot, almost noiselessly. So, when she let out a shocked exclamation, Bipasha almost fell forward onto the sharp *bonti*.

'What have you done? What have you done?' she kept repeating, while Bipasha sucked at her thumb, which she had slit on the blade of the bonti when she had started.

Finally, she turned around and in a weary voice asked, 'What is it now. What have I done?'

Without giving a direct answer, the old lady stood near the steel thali on which Bipasha had made two neat piles of potatoes and spring onion greens, and kept on muttering her shock and disbelief.

'Now I'll have to buy a new bonti. My niramish bonti is gone! This one I had found in Kalighat Market, the only one I had been satisfied with. Now I'll have to buy another one. What a waste of money! What an unnecessary expense!'

Puti heard the commotion and joined her mother. Now they both stood accusingly over Bipasha, who was racking her brains and sucking her thumb from which the blood wouldn't stop oozing. She knew she must suck out all of it, or it might not heal for days.

After a while Puti asked, 'What is it Ma, what happened?'

This opened a fresh floodgate of resentment.

'Look at what she's done. She's chopped the spring onions on my niramish bonti. The brand new one we bought from Kalighat, from the last *Rather Mela*. And it was so beautifully sharp. I had really loved it.'

'You mean, spring onion greens are amish?' Bipasha asked in astonishment.

'What did you think—its niramish?' Puti said sarcastically.

'Naturally. It's only logical. Look,' Bipasha held out the thali, 'they look green, don't they?'

'So, you're going to teach me now, is it? Now I have to learn from you what is amish and what is niramish.'

Bipasha was now more angry than confused. She had had enough of this circus, she decided. 'Then why were they kept in the fridge?' she retorted belligerently. I thought only vegetarian stuff were kept in the fridge. If these were not niramish, how will you touch the rest of the stuff in the fridge?'

'I think she comes from a Muslim family,' her mother-in-law said, with her lips contorted in disgust. 'If she doesn't know the difference, she can't be descended from Brahmins.'

This was meant to be the ultimate insult. Bipasha leapt up sharply. Puti realised it had gone a bit too far.

'Actually, some things, like eggs, can be kept in the fridge as long as they are whole,' she said in a somewhat conciliatory tone. 'When you break an egg, it becomes amish. Similarly, when you chop the spring onions, they become amish.'

Bipasha pulled down her sari covering her head, in a gesture of defiance. Then, throwing the extra yard over her shoulder sharply, like a 60s actress, she squared her shoulders.

'You keep your niramish and amish. You keep your stupid customs. I'm off. You do your own chopping and cooking. I am through with all this nonsense.'

As she made for the door, her mother-in-law jumped aside so she wouldn't be touched.

'You wash your hands before touching anything else in the house,' she warned. 'And where do you think you're going, who's going to cook that stuff now?' Puti has her periods and can't go into the kitchen . . . and I can't touch it. . . .'

In the heat of her first anger, Bipasha threw her suitcase on her bed and started to pack. She began throwing in her things haphazardly. Saris, nighties, toiletries, and a box of casual jewellery that she had kept in her almirah. . . .

Then her eyes fell on the wall clock. It was almost seven. Her husband would be home within half an hour, maybe sooner. What would he say about this development? Would he take her side? Or would he be disappointed with her?

Her own mother, how would *she* feel? Her daughter is back from her *shashurbari* within six months of marriage. What would her relatives say? So much had gone into the wedding, good wishes, blessings, financial help, those tears in the eyes of loved ones, when she had bent to touch their feet before leaving for her new home.

Most of all, how would she live the rest of her life with herself, remembering that she had quitted over a silly issue like spring onion greens?

Bipasha thought of her two younger sisters. They had always made her feel like a dependable and responsible sister. Would they have the same respect for her now?

Slowly, her anger was replaced by anxiety. Who would take care of her husband? She had already grown attached to him.

He was a nice man to be married to. Suppose he felt hurt about this whole thing and never forgave her?

Slowly, Bipasha started putting back the things. Back went the clothes into the cupboard, the toiletries into the dresser, the jewellery into the safe.

There was no one in the kitchen. The old lady must be in her room with Puti. The steel thali was still lying on the floor; the two neat mounds slightly messed up by the impact of the bonti, when it had fallen over sideways. . . .

At dinner, Bipasha's husband took a second helping of the spring onion curry.

'This is very tasty,' he said.

Then he looked at his mother, who sat at her own separate table having her two chapattis with a white potato curry.

'Ma, your *bou* cooks real well,' he said. 'Have you tried this new spring onion thing?'

Eldest Brother's Wife

FOR THE THREE SISTERS, THIS WAS THE FIFTH PROSPECTIVE bride they had come to see for their eldest brother—all the previous ones having been rejected for their dark complexion. But this girl was stunningly fair, something that rated highest in their count. It was a family obsession. No matter how perfect the other features were, it would all add up to nothing if she was dark. Their mother was proud of her fair-complexioned daughters and she would have nothing less for her son.

'What's your name?' Himani, the eldest of the three sisters asked.

'Gauri,' the girl promptly replied, as if she were answering an oral exam question.

'Ah, the name matches the complexion!' Himani remarked, in an effort to relax the tense atmosphere in the room.

Everyone smiled politely, acknowledging the compliment, except Gauri herself, who stood expressionless, restlessly shifting from one foot to another, unconcerned of the glare of scrutiny of the three sisters. Then, in the uncomfortable silence when

Himani was searching for a suitable question to ask, Gauri looked around and declared, 'I am sixteen years old,' as if she was answering the next question on the list.

There was a nervous giggle from Gauri's aunt, who adjusted the sari covering her head and glanced at her mother-in-law, Gauri's grandmother. Taking the cue, the ascetic-looking old lady rose gracefully.

'Why don't you come and help me serve the sweets,' she said kindly to Gauri and ushered her out of the room.

'Our child is very simple at heart,' Gauri's aunt said almost apologetically trying to erase any adverse impression that Gauri may have created by her unsolicited statement.

'You see, her mother, my sister-in-law died after her birth and she was brought up by her grandmother and me.'

Soon, Gauri and her grandmother returned, balancing plates full of sweets for the sisters. As was customary, the visitors protested.

'Too many sweets!' Himani exclaimed.

'Oh no, it's nothing much. Please do have them,' the aunt said, handing a plate each to the sisters, personally.

Bela, the middle sister noted how uncomfortable Gauri seemed to be in the wide-bordered, crisp *tangail* sari, which she tried not to trip on, as she carried in the plates. If she was sixteen, she was the same age as her. This interested Bela, because she couldn't imagine herself in Gauri's role, at her age. Nor could she imagine herself wearing a sari and becoming a bride. With her school final exams coming up and all the plans of going to college, such thoughts were farthest from her mind. It also struck her as odd that eldest brother, who was thirty-one, might get married to someone as young as sixteen. Well, maybe she was lying about her age. Mother said that they all did this because in the marriage market, it was safe to be as far behind twenty as possible, as the moment they crossed twenty, they were considered old hags.

The youngest sister Koli put down her plate of sweets with a grimace. She didn't like sweets and she also felt a little restless in the stuffy room full of ladies in stiff, starched saris. As was the case, her Sunday evening had been spoilt. Normally, she would be with her friends from the neighbouring houses, playing ludo or carom. Instead, here she was sitting and staring at the faces of strangers and listening to their small talk. When she had refused going, mother said that it didn't look nice for eldest sister to go alone on a social engagement such as this, and hence she had had to dress up in the awful pink, frilled dacron dress that eldest sister's mother-in-law had gifted to her on last Puja, and had to tag along reluctantly. She had been sworn to secrecy by mother and eldest sister, so that eldest brother didn't know that his marriage was being plotted. Apparently, he didn't want to get married because he thought he didn't earn enough money to support a wife. But mother and eldest sister worried that he was getting too old. They were confident that if a beautiful, young girl was found, he might just be tempted to tie the knot. Till then, however, she had to keep her mouth shut, because, as everyone was aware, eldest brother was short tempered and he might just blow up if he learnt what was going on without his consent. Not that he was mean or anything, in fact, he was a kind-hearted and generous man and didn't like hurting people. He was actually being considerate towards any girl, who might be considered for the marriage, not knowing his financial condition.

Koli was fond of her eldest brother, who took her to the zoo and the museum and also to watch Walt Disney films. Because her father had died when she was a baby, her eldest brother made up for her father.

Himani swallowed the last sweet and kept down her plate. She had been watching Gauri and marvelling at her complexion. She did look a little young, considering eldest brother's age. But did a man's age matter? In fact, the younger the girl was, it would be easier for her to adjust to the in-laws. Being an orphan and having been brought up in a lower-middle-class family, meant that she wouldn't have very high expectations either. No, everything seemed perfect, except that these people didn't seem very well off and probably wouldn't be able to muster up much dowry. Anyway, first things first, she reasoned. Complexion was the most important thing and she intended to check it out properly. After all, she was the one, mother was depending on, as she was the only married sister and therefore, experienced in such matters.

'Have you applied any powder on your face?' she asked point blank, looking at Gauri with narrowed eyes.

Gauri had been sitting, staring at her toes and wriggling them, having been told by grandma not to speak unless asked to. Her mind was now focused on the plate of sweets Koli had barely touched. She had nibbled at the *rasogolla*, after much coaxing from Gauri's aunt and the pale yellow *chamcham* lay beside the dark brown *gulabjaam*, making her mouth water. She had to focus hard on her toes and swallow, to keep her mind off the plate. There were a few extra pieces that she had bought with the money grandma had given her. But she knew that with her younger cousins around, she didn't have a chance. They had probably already got to them.

'Answer!' her aunt hissed into her ear and pushed her with her elbow.

'Has she applied make-up on her face?' Himani asked again, this time addressing the aunt.

The lady adjusted her hood again, 'Oh no, our Gauri doesn't have to use that kind of stuff. She is naturally fair.'

'Let me see?' Himani gestured for Gauri to move closer to her.

But Gauri's mind just couldn't detach itself from the plate of sweets and she was oblivious to the fact that she was being addressed. She was hungry. All the extra work she had done today, the tidying of the sitting room, walking down to Kalibabu's shop all the way to the main road in order to buy the sweets, had worked up her appetite. Normally, there was nothing much to eat between lunch and dinner. Her cousins, who went to school, were given half glasses of milk before they did their homework. But Gauri would be lucky to be given a small bowl of *muri*. Now, however, the sight of the sweets lying there, wasted because it was obvious the little girl in the pink dress wasn't interested, was making it worse.

Suddenly, a push from aunt made her jolt back to her senses. Aunt's strong and rough hand gripped her elbow and propelled her towards the aristocratic-looking lady, wearing gold-rimmed spectacles. As she crossed the plate of sweets, perched on the small cane stool, placed beside the girl's chair, the temptation became too much for her to bear. Gauri suddenly bent down and in one swoop, picked up the gulabjaam from the pool of syrup and put it into her mouth. It didn't take a second for the soft, syrupy ball to plummet down her throat, into her stomach. Her stomach groaned audibly with pleasure and she would have gone for the chamcham as well but aunt's rough hand fell on her arm in a hard slap from behind and before she realised, she was looking through the spectacles of the aristocratic lady, whose eyes were boring into her face from an inch away. The thick glasses made her eyes look so big that it scared Gauri and she averted her gaze. Next thing she knew, her cheeks and nose were being rubbed like a blackboard, with a handkerchief and it was hurting her skin.

'How could you have done such a shameful thing?' eldest brother roared like a lion in rage and paced up and down, as the three sisters and their mother cowered. Himani, the target of his tirade, shot an angry glance at Koli, who had unintentionally blurted out the incident in a moment of weakness.

'Rubbed a girl's face to see if she had used powder?'

He spread his hands disbelievingly and paused, trying to absorb the implications.

'How uncultured can one get? I don't believe that my own sister did this. Shame on you! What would father have said if he was alive? I just don't know how to make up for this act. It is bad enough that you went behind my back, knowing very well that I had no intentions of getting married now. Then, over and above that, you went and doubled the wrong by doing this uncivilised thing!'

He paced for a whole hour, while his mother and sisters prayed he would fall into the trap. Finally, when he came up to them and said, 'Get in touch with the pundit—I want to know the earliest possible dates.' His mother fell on her knees in front of the family God and thanked Him with tears in her eyes, simultaneously mourning the fact that her husband wasn't there to share this happy day with her. Himani, though relieved, silently twisted Koli's ears for letting her down.

'Remember,' warned eldest brother, 'nothing elaborate. I have no money to waste. I'm doing this just to make up for your stupid act.'

After a small reception on the night of the *boubhaat*, it was finally time for the eldest brother and his newly-wed wife to go to bed together, for the first time. Gauri had been tutored by Himani, now her eldest sister-in-law, about eldest brother's nature and his habits, so that nothing might surprise or shock her. After the new bride had been helped to change into comfortable clothes and eldest brother subjected to some restrained teasing, which he immediately put a stop to with a frown of disapproval, the couple were allowed to retire to their room. The women however, huddled together, joking and giggling about the prospect of their volatile, short-tempered and down-to-earth eldest brother being romantic for a change. Soon, they dozed off, fantasising about the various possibilities.

The loud bang of the door woke them up and the lurking fear in their minds immediately transformed into panic, when they heard eldest brother's loud swearing. Next moment he appeared in their doorway in his underwear and a face so red that for a moment they thought he was ill.

'So, you people even rubbed her cheeks to see if she was wearing make-up, did you?' Menacingly, he advanced towards them.

'But you didn't happen to examine her mouth, did you? *Did you*?' he exploded.

The sight that greeted them as they slowly gathered around the doorway, made them exclaim in horror. The new bride sat on the flower-bedecked bed, her hair dishevelled, her face streaked with the remnants of her bridal make-up and her mouth broken up into a toothless, crumpled hollow. In her hand, she held a complete set of dentures that looked as perfect as a dentist's model.

'Dear Lord!' Himani shrieked, 'I had marvelled at how beautiful her teeth were!'

Then, quickly moving to her bedside, trying her best to shield her from everyone's view, she said with pity, 'Silly girl! Why did you have to take them off on your wedding night?'

Gandharaj Lime

IT WAS NOW QUITE EVIDENT THAT THE GRAND OLD PATRIARCH wouldn't last out the day. He had taken a turn for the worse since last night. The doctor said that the swelling of the legs was a bad sign and they should be prepared for the ultimate.

All his eleven sons and daughters, daughters-in-law and grandchildren had gathered in the small flat since yesterday night. The sons-in-law had kept vigil through the night, and then left for their offices in the morning.

The women looked awful. They had practically gone without sleep, as the massive body of the dying man had heaved and pitched trying to breathe. Now, as his favourite three-year-old grandson was carried into his room by his mother, he lay like a dead ship, without any signs of life.

'Say goodbye to *Dadu*. Like this,' she tried to fold little Prosenjit's tiny hands into a prayer-like gesture.

'Say, Dadu, pranaam.' But the boy, usually inseparable from his grandfather, refused to even look at him and kept his head obstinately fixed on his mother's shoulder. Finally, she gave up.

'I think he knows,' she told everyone later. 'I think he senses that Dadu can't hear him.'

The flat was now full of neighbours and friends from the locality. They stood around, wanting to say or do something that would be meaningful. The old man's wife was under focus. They stared at her haggard face from which the vermillion mark of marriage shone with an incongruous brightness. They looked at her with an eye of sympathy, but having no appropriate way of expressing what they felt, just sighed to themselves.

The sons had their breakfast in the dining room, looking drawn and unkempt. Anaadi, the Bihari servant managed to make some, as the women remained with their mother-in-law and were busy keeping the children under control.

'I think we should buy some good fish today, for Ma,' Ajitesh said. He was the youngest of the brothers and being unmarried, still lived with his parents. Obviously, it was a detail the other brothers had overlooked. Being married and having their own families, they felt more like guests in their father's house.

'Good idea, good idea,' they all agreed. 'Of course!' Hurriedly they emptied their pockets, glad to be able to contribute something.

The old man was holding on. The friends and neighbours left, wondering how long it would be—the waiting. Strange though it was, the family did all the routine things they did everyday. It was difficult because there was only one bathroom and twenty-five people, including the children. For an hour or so, after Ajitesh left with Anaadi for the market, they all bathed and dressed and talked of normal things, avoiding the issue at hand. And though it was the old man who lay dying, everyone fussed over his wife, she being perceived as the real victim of this drama, the woman, who would be left with half her life, after the old man was gone.

They helped her bathe and get dressed, making her wear an exceptionally dark coloured sari, as if it mattered now. The eldest daughter-in-law daubed her forefinger in the bowl of sindur and made a perfect bindi on her mother-in-law's forehead and then with the base of a comb dipped in the same vermillion powder, marked out her hair parting. She did this like a sacred ritual, meant to keep her husband alive. The old lady however, went about it like a numb person, the desert wind blowing up against her mind. The wail that was to come soon, was already gathering momentum in her weak body.

The morning became frenetic as soon as Ajitesh returned with the grocery. Accompanied by Anaadi, he had scoured the local markets for every kind of fish that Ma liked. He had even gone up to the Sealdah Market to get some fresh hilsa—the king of all fishes for East Bengalis. He was the family expert, having grown up in Dhaka, in East Bengal, a land dominated by rivers and where fishing was a way of life. Today however, was exceptional because it wasn't the time of the year for hilsa, which became tasty only during the monsoons when their supply was more abundant and there were no eggs inside the fish. But it couldn't be helped. He had to do with whatever was available now, in the middle of summer. Come monsoon, Ma would be a widow and not be able to eat fish.

The entire morning, while the old man lay dying, his breath now only an undetectable whisper, the kitchen became the centre of activity. Anaadi scaled, cleaned and chopped the fish. There was a whole five kg rohu, two whole hilsas, two kgs of galda prawns and two kgs of silvery white parshey. The daughters-in-law, their saris covering their heads, as they were at their in-laws' house, got busy grinding turmeric, coriander, cumin and mustard. Ajitesh hovered over them, instructing them—*doi machh* with rohu, hilsa with mustard paste and prawns with coconut milk. By afternoon the house smelled like a marriage house with the fragrance of basmati rice mingling with ghee and spices. The only thing missing was the fragrance of flowers and the sound of the shehnai.

The other member of the family, who hadn't left the patriarch's room since yesterday, was Baby, the youngest of the five daughters. She had always been the lost and forgotten one. Nobody would suspect that she was twenty years old; she looked so frail and girlish, also she was deaf in her right ear, nobody knew why. Baby, the weak one—the one who had come after the old man had retired from active service. Her birthday coincided with the birth of their first grandchild. They were so embarrassed of her that she was seldom introduced to strangers. In fact, when they had to leave Dhaka in a hurry before the Partition, they had barely remembered to pack her up with their other belongings, but she loved her father like a desperately loyal pet. Now, she stuck to the huge bedpost like a fly, unblinking, taking in every belaboured breath of the old man with her entire being. It was as if she was dying with him.

The dining room floor had been swept and mopped and small rugs were placed on the floor along the walls with the freshly washed, gleaming banana leaves laid out before each rug.

There were tiny mounds of salt and a green chilli on the upper right hand corner of each banana leaf. Earthen glasses filled with water had been placed by the side of the leaf plates, which already had puddles under them. These glasses always leaked, no matter how carefully you checked them before buying and Anaadi kept mopping the floor and wiping the glasses. The daughters-in-law, gleaming with sweat, dabbed their faces with the ends of their saris, waiting for their husbands and mother-in-law to take their places. The sisters-in-law would wait for now and join their *boudis* later. They were ready to serve the food, with the help of Anaadi, who would carry the heavy bowls from the kitchen. There was a sense of urgency in the air now. Ma had to eat before anything happened to the old man.

The sons, daughters and daughters-in-law waited, surrounding the old lady as she sat down with a sigh. She tilted her earthen glass and rinsed her hand with a little water—a ritual she still continued though her children now washed their hands in the basin, ever since they came to Calcutta. Anaadi brought in the daal but she waved it away.

'Get the fish first,' Ajitesh ordered. Today the daal wasn't important. She would be having daal for the rest of her life, but she would be having fish for the last time today, so it was important not to waste her appetite with daal.

The eldest daughter-in-law bent down to serve the rohu. The combined aroma of garam masala, ghee and yoghurt hit everyone's nostrils and made their mouth water. But before she could ladle out the first helping, the old lady called out to Anaadi.

'Is there a slice of gandharaj lime?'

Anaadi clucked his tongue and slapped his forehead. His mistake! He knew how much the old lady loved gandharaj. Everyday, during the summer when it was available and was really juicy and fragrant, he never forgot to buy some, along with the vegetable. How could he have forgotten? Before anyone could say anything, he said, 'I'll get it in a minute,' and rushed out of the door.

The nearest market was about ten minutes away but Anaadi had been known to cover the distance in five minutes, when something was needed urgently.

'Idiot!' Ajitesh fumed. 'His mind is always on something else.'

The old lady sighed again. She waited, with her hand on the banana leaf, away from her body, because she had touched the rice on her plate. She was strict about these rules. Once she touched anything containing cooked rice, she couldn't use the same hand to touch anything or anyone, without washing her hand. Everyone sat and waited with her.

Ajitesh fidgeted. He was an energetic and restless man. He liked getting things done and he equated physical energy with manliness. He thought of *Calcuttans* as effeminate because they were not known to be physically very active people.

'Where's the stupid idiot gone?'

He rose from the rug.

'Calm down, *thakurpo*,' the eldest daughter-in-law said soothingly, 'He has just left.'

She was the only one who exercised some sort of authority over him. Even his parents had never been able to control him.

It was the old lady who heard it first. She turned her head and held it alert, in the direction of the old man's room.

'Ma . . . aa . . . aa . . . !'

Baby's scream rose like the high pitched note of a flute. When they reached the room, her knuckles had gone white; she was squeezing the bedpost so hard with her bony hands. Her mouth was stuck in a scream, though the sound had escaped. The terrified expression on her face said that she had seen it all, all by herself. while the others were in the dining room. She had heard his last breath come and go off into the emptiness of the room. In the mysterious way, when even children know when life disappears, Baby had realised that her father was dead.

The wails of the women woke up little Prosenjit who was asleep in the next room. His mother ran in, picked him up and rushed back. The old woman now lay with her head on her dead husband's feet, wailing as if her heart would break. 'Why did you leave me behind,' she kept repeating. 'Why didn't you take me with you?'

The neighbours had returned soon after the wails had broken the silence of the afternoon. They pressed their mouth with the palms of their hands and fought back their tears, as the old woman's lamentations cut through their hearts.

Ajitesh had already left the scene. He was on his way to a neighbour's house to use their phone. There was no time to waste. He had to call the doctor and start organising the funeral. He bumped into Anaadi on his way out. He was panting, as he had been running all the way from the market. He was holding the gandharaj lime in a piece of newspaper.

'*Çhhod da*,' he said, his voice breaking into tears, 'Now, what will I do with all the fish?'

Small Change

GORA CHATTERJEE JUMPED ONTO THE MINI BUS WITH AN ENERGY that was incongruous in the midday heat of summer. Almost immediately, he lost his foothold, as the bus lurched forward and he had to scramble for the nearest empty seat. It was the aisle side of a seat already occupied by a half-asleep, grouchy-looking middle-aged man. Had Gora not been in an elated state of mind, he would never have opted to sit there. He hated aisle seats because when the bus grew crowded, the standing passengers tended to press onto the person seated on the side, with their sweating bodies. But today, it didn't matter to him. He was in a celebratory mood, having just received his letter of promotion and a substantial raise in salary. Life seemed hunky-dory. In fact, he had taken time off during lunch to go home and surprise his wife with the good news and also two tickets to Goa that he had bought, planning a nice holiday in mind. That's why he was in the minibus, braving the midday heat—only the lure of her happy smile had pulled him out of his comfortable, air-conditioned office.

As he settled down to his half of the seat, Gora couldn't avoid a sigh of satisfaction. But it was short-lived. The old man now changed his posture, kicking Gora on his left shin and then proceeded to snore. As he turned to protest, the striking resemblance of the man's face with his own late father made him stop and stare. There was a look of disdain on his unkempt face and all the memories of his unhappy childhood came flooding back. His father's scorn for money; their resultant poverty and the way his mother had to sell off all her jewellery in order to put Gora through school and college . . . he had vowed that he would never live like his father and had worked hard and planned every step of his life, to get out of the rut. Now hardly thirty-five, he was already earning a four-figure salary; owned a small second-hand car; had booked a two-bedroomed flat in Salt Lake and had bought a Life Insurance policy. Gora was proud of his achievements. His enemies said that he was vain and obsessed. But Gora couldn't care less. 'Ruthless planning is what has got me where I am today,' he thought proudly, straightening his Zodiac tie, which looked a little ostentatious in the midst of the shabby minibus crowd. 'Absolutely nothing can be achieved without planning,' he repeated to himself, thinking of his father again.

The conductor boy came and stood with his legs straddled. Gora fished out his leather wallet. He flicked through the crisp, new notes he had collected from the bank. Well, of course there were no small notes. He had forgotten to ask for any. After all, he didn't normally travel by bus. It was only because he had to give his car for servicing that day. He took out a ten rupee note and held it out to the boy, knowing very well what his reaction was going to be. The boy extended his hand, and then withdrew it immediately.

'Dada, give me a one-rupee note. I can't give you so much change,' he protested.

Gora noticed the curious glances that followed. They must be wondering how such a specimen had landed in their midst. He knew that people who travelled by public transport considered themselves as part of one vast fraternity—the classes who couldn't afford their own car. And when someone obviously belonging to the privileged minority boarded a bus, it became equivalent to trespassing. It was not that Gora wasn't aware of the rules. It was scrawled very visibly on the panel facing them. 'NO CHANGE GIVEN ABOVE TWO RUPEES.' He realised, he had slipped.

'Sorry, brother, I don't have a one rupee.'

Gora tried to sound as apologetic as possible, hoping he would make an exception in this case.

'Two rupees will do,' the boy said in a tired voice and moved away to the next row. He had no time to solve passenger problems.

For the first time that morning, Gora felt really stupid. He looked around desperately, wondering if he should swallow his pride and ask someone for change.

'Dada seems to have a lot of money. Why doesn't he charter a plane?' some smartass snickered from behind.

Suddenly the sleeping man beside Gora seemed to be the only option. At least he was old and harmless.

'Dada!' he said, in a low voice. The man woke up with a start and stared at the ten rupee note that Gora held in front of him. 'Do you have some change?'

The old man blinked, then reluctantly sat up and reached inside the pocket of his frayed kurta. 'Ten rupees!' he grumbled, 'How can I give you so much change?'

'Of course, you couldn't,' Gora thought to himself, 'You're exactly like my father! You even look like him. Probably believe in plain living—high thinking, whatever that means. You'll probably even die like him, without insurance, without medical assistance, because you won't have a penny in the bank. Probably believe in destiny, too.'

'Ten rupees!' he mumbled again, foraging inside his pocket.

'I would be very grateful,' Gora said humbly.

He looked on hopefully as the man took out a bunch of loose coins from his right pocket and put it in his left hand. They were all ten paisa coins. He fished out the second handful and held out both palms towards Gora.

'Count,' he ordered, briefly.

'This is ridiculous,' Gora thought as he started to count, gingerly picking up one coin at a time. When he finished counting two rupees, his left palm had a mound of precariously balanced change that was in danger of falling off any moment, as the bus was lurching viciously, everytime the driver changed gears. He looked on helplessly, as the old man dug out some more ten paisa coins.

'Dada, don't you have any bigger change?'

Gora was now quite desperate but the look that the man gave him, said everything. As if to spite him, he now sat up and put his hands on his lap.

'That's it. That's all the change I have,' he said with finality.

Gora knew that he didn't have to count anymore. The entire bunch wouldn't add up to more than four rupees. 'Sorry I bothered you,' he said a little coldly, 'but this is not enough.'

He extended his hands full of coin carefully towards the old man. With disgust written all over his face, the man stood up and positioned himself sideways, gesturing Gora to place the money back into his pocket.

The busboy approached again. It was now just one stop away from his destination. Gora stood up and pushed the ten rupee note into the boy's hand. 'Keep the change,' he said and hurried towards the exit. Gora could sense the looks that followed him. He had never felt so embarrassed in his life. If only the bus would slow down a bit, he could jump off and walk the rest of the way.

'Dada, take your ticket, at least,' the busboy shouted, as he punched it hurriedly.

The minibus was now veering towards the pavement. 'To hell with the ticket,' Gora thought. He didn't want to hear any of those stupid comments again. He leaned out from the footboard, trying to measure the distance between the bus and the road. Then, he jumped.

Gora came out of his unconsciousness feeling as if he had no body. His eyes tried to focus but he kept drifting away into sleep. Finally, he recognised his wife, who was looking down at him anxiously.

'Where am I?' he managed to articulate.

'You're in hospital,' she whispered. Even in his drugged condition he could make out that she was crying.

'I can't remember,' he said with difficulty. 'What happened?'

'You fell out of the bus.'

'The bus . . .' He mumbled and drifted off again.

Then, just as his wife thought he had fallen asleep, he opened his eyes and said, 'There were two tickets in my shirt pocket . . . to Goa.'

His wife sat still, crying.

Gora tried to lift his hand and wipe away her tears. She doesn't know, he thought. She doesn't know the good news. But his hands, like his whole body, seemed dead, especially his legs. . . .

'Why are you crying?' He asked with great effort. 'I got a promotion. . . .'

Sobbing loudly, she reached out and touched his face tenderly, 'We can't go anywhere now. They had to amputate your leg . . .' she broke down.

Gora dreamt that he was in a classroom which was inside a bus. Benches were placed neatly one after the other, he was sitting along with many uniformed students, facing a grouchy, dishevelled old man.

The man lifted his cane and shouted, 'Which one of you sons-of-pigs forgot to bring change?'

The other faces around him blurred and faded; only he remained. He stood up fearfully and inched away towards the exit.

The old man moved towards him with the raised cane.

'I . . . I . . . wasn't supposed to be in the bus. . . .' He babbled, stammering in fear. 'M . . . m . . . my car was in the garage. . . .' Gora pleaded.

But the old man kept swishing the cane menacingly, as he moved closer and closer.

'You should have planned ahead,' he roared, 'You should have known your destiny!'

As he brought down the cane, Gora saw himself slipping and falling over the edge. . . .

Wrong Entrance

Everyone who had come to Shadashib Banerjee's daughter's wedding had gone home talking about the bridegroom's good looks. In his starched and neatly pleated cotton dhoti, cream coloured *garad punjaabi* and embroidered leather *nagras*, all presented from the bride's side, Manoranjan Chatterjee looked more like a Westerner. Yes, they all agreed, looking at him as he sat in front of the ritual fire, crowned with the *shola*. He looked like a *jamaai*, worth calling by that name.

His family too came under admiring stares. They were looked up to for their elegance and their taste. His sisters, decked in their Benarasis and gold jewellery, looked more like Greek goddesses draped in Indian costumes. 'Complexions bursting out,' that's how they were admired in Bengali, by their guests. But the morning when the *tatwa* had arrived Shadashib Banerjee's place, for the bride's turmeric shower, it had disappointed not only the guests but also Sadashib Banerjee.

The women of the family and the neighbourhood had eagerly gathered to greet the arrival of the customary gift from the groom's house, announced by blowing of conch shells and ululation. People had expected Shadashib Babu's daughter's in-laws to put up a grand show, and that they would keep up with his respectable status. After all, the tatwa that was going to be sent to the groom's house on the next day's boubhaat, was already being talked about as being the most opulent they had seen in their lifetimes. The bamboo trays full of beautiful saris for each member of the groom's family had been selected by Shadashib Babu personally and so were the dhoti and kurta pieces for the male members. Then there were shining brass utensils in all shapes and sizes—large *ghadas*, *kalshis*, *danis*, and sets of thalis, glasses and bowls—enough to throw a royal banquet. Large amount of sweets and varieties of fishes had been ordered in advance and everything was to be displayed for the admiration of acquaintances before sending it off with blowing of conch shells. Shadashib Banerjee came from an aristocratic and wealthy merchant family of Baghbazar and everyone knew that his only daughter's wedding would be as lavish as it could get.

What they hadn't expected was the apology of a tatwa sent by the bridegroom's side. People started to stream in from the morning, to participate in the turmeric bath ritual of the bride-to-be, the inaugural event of the three-day-long marriage ceremony. Receiving the tatwa with enthusiasm is an important part of the proceedings and everyone was expecting a grand show. But all their expectations were belied when they saw just two of the bridegroom's siblings arriving in a taxi with the turmeric and sari for the bride. The small size of the fish and the tiny tray of sweets further deflated the onlookers; they had already started whispering amongst themselves with an expression of surprise written on their faces. Shadashib Babu was thoroughly embarrassed and he immediately sent out his servants to the market to buy enough fish to supplement what came from the groom's side, so that they could feed all the guests in the afternoon.

❦

Shadashib Babu had not chosen Manoranjan Chatterjee for his wealth, or for his lack of it. Nor was it entirely for his stunning good looks. He had seen something rare in the young man—a contagious energy and an eagerness for life that he found lacking in most young Bengali men since India's Independence. Manoranjan had a magnetic personality and a pleasant character. The conviction behind his ideas and the progressiveness of his thoughts attracted Shadashib Babu, who placed his daughter's life in the context of the new, Independent India and not merely as a limited motif within the typical Bengali socio-economic pattern. He had realised, wisely, that the future happiness of his daughter lay in not what she inherited, but in what she and her husband could create for themselves, together. Hence, he had overlooked Manoranjan's lower-middle-class background and the fact this young man supported a large family, with ageing and ailing parents, young, unmarried sisters and had no property or bank balance to fall back upon. He whole-heartedly admired the pluck and courage of a politically displaced family, trying to reestablish itself in a foreign city, after leaving behind their sprawling house in Dhaka, and their prosperous living. He appreciated this man's restlessness and courage to try out a new destiny and leave his mark in the history of this nation. Shadashiv Banerjee had liked him, instantly. Oh, yes! And he had never stopped talking about him since.

More than anything else, Shadashib Babu admired 'style'. Little things in the way a person conducted himself, mattered greatly, he felt, in the way his life was going to turn out in the end. He had rejected scores of other prospective matches for such reasons. For instance, the son of another very wealthy businessman was spurned because his father had plucked a flower in his garden, without taking his permission. He thought that was gross. Such a man would have no finesse, no aesthetic sensibility, he had judged.

Then there was the case of a family who had come to *see* his daughter and the only questions they had asked her were regarding what *phodons* she was supposed to put into various native Bengali dishes. This proposal was rejected outright. Their conversation was suggesting that all his daughter was expected to do in their house was to cook, which wasn't the kind of life he had visualised for his 'BA first-class-first' daughter.

Neither had he considered, even for a moment, a man whose lawyer father kept on interrogating his daughter about what choices she would make in difficult situations like, if her mother-in-law was on fire, and her father-in-law had fallen into a well, whom would she first rush to save? Shadashib thought that the family had serious psychological problems.

He had even rejected some perfectly eligible young men too. One was rejected because he had eaten up all twelve rasgollas from the serving plate and another for mentioning his toilet habits in course of the conversation.

Relatives and friends had started to tease the poor girl that she would never be able to get married with such a finicky father, always busy finding flaws. But finally Manoranjan Chatterjee arrived, literally like the proverbial knight on a white horse and conquered everyone's hearts. Shadashib Babu was charmed by everything about Manoranjan, his looks, his personality, his habits, his job prospects and most of all, his attitude towards life. 'Class'—that was the term he kept on using, with reference to this young man. He was always dressed handsomely with his striped or checked shirts, perfectly tailored trousers, hair slicked back from a noble forehead with Brylcream—like contemporary Hollywood heroes and either wearing moccasins or strapped sandals—never 'chappals'. Shadashib Babu detested men who wore pumps with dhotis, or chappals with trousers. On the day he visited the Chatterjee's flat in Bhowanipore, Manoranjan pleasantly surprised him by wearing kurta and pyjamas and was relieved to learn that he too, hated the habit some men from East Bengal had, that of wearing *lungis* at home.

He also noticed how the modest drawing room had been

aesthetically furnished with embroidered cushion covers, laces on armrests and fresh flowers in a vase, things that middle-class Bengalis tended to be sloppy about. He was most impressed by the refreshments offered him. He thought it was unique that instead of the traditional Bengali sweets, the man had taken the trouble to get pastries from Flury's and chicken patties from Nahoun's in New Market.

So, when the 'turmeric shower tatwa' turned out to be a bit of an anti-climax, though flustered, Shadashib Babu did his best to cover up for his son-in-law. He took the blame on himself, saying that it was he, who had advised them not to send an elaborate tatwa.

However, all was forgiven when people got to see the bridegroom. Everyone was busy admiring him, 'No wonder Shadashib Babu had fallen for this boy!'

'Truly a prince charming! Lucky Shadashib Babu,' Shadashib Banerjee grinned in satisfaction and congratulated himself for being choosey.

It was the first visit of the newly-wed girl to her parents' house after the marriage and luckily it coincided with her birthday. It was celebration time in the Banerjee home. Her friends and family were eagerly awaiting this opportunity to learn more about the shaheb jamaai. She was still decked in her wedding finery, she seemed to be the same except the pinkish blush that was partly because of the sindur that was dripping very becomingly onto her nose and forehead (from its liberal application on her hair parting by her husband, during the wedding ceremony) and partly due to the coyness of a bride.

The bride sat cross-legged and relaxed amidst her old and familiar and revelled in the attention. They treated her like a goddess, touching her with curious reverence, as if she had crossed over into some privileged zone. Oh, they were dying to learn about every single moment of her existence with jamai babu ever since the day she got married. A volley of questions followed, 'What is *he* like?', 'What are his habits?', 'How did he behave with you?' She revealed only what she felt was appropriate and avoided shyly what she felt was private.

After a few hours of probing, they got a clear picture about jamai babu. Though he followed the usual Bengali lifestyle, he was quite progressive by nature and was influenced by Western ideas. He looked handsome in suit and tie when he went to office. He loved eating out. He had a gramophone and listened to Western music, though he hummed Rabindra Sangeet and *adhunik* songs in the bathroom. Yes, they had gone for the night show of a Hollywood movie—only the two of them—not with the sisters, as it was an adult movie. So, what did he give her on her birthday? He had wished her Happy Birthday in the morning. That's all? Well, he did say he had a surprise for her and that she'll get it today.

What was it going to be? What was it going to be?

'Has to be something classy,' someone commented.

'Not like the turmeric shower tatwa, I hope,' someone else joked.

'You'll see, you'll see,' Shadashib Babu said proudly. He too had started feeling excited about it.

☙

It was a tiring journey; the bride was heading for a shower. Walking towards the bathroom with her clothes hung over her shoulder, she was lost anticipating about the gift her husband would give her. She was smiling to herself as she threaded her way through the kids running here and there. The house was full of relatives but she was missing him. It was strange, that this house, where she had grown up and her relatives, all seemed to have become distant. She hadn't mentioned to them how small her in-laws' flat was, how the rest of the family squeezed into one bedroom, because now the other one was theirs, and how small the bathroom was, so small that one found it difficult to change clothes inside.

Bolting the wooden door of the bathroom she thought about how she had been using this spacious bathroom all her life. She hung the clothes she was carrying, on the wall hanger and took off all her ornaments one by one and kept them on the glass rack over the basin. Then, like she had done since childhood, checked the door-latch of the sweeper's exit. Sometimes the servants forgot to lock it after the sweeper left. There was a spiral staircase leading from that door to the backyard, a feature seen in most of the old North Calcutta houses.

Just as she was about to step under the shower, there was a knock on the door. At first she thought it came from that door which led into the house that is from where she had entered.

'*Ke*?' she asked, surprised.

There was a muted scraping sound, but this time she felt it came from the other door, the sweeper's exit that led to the backyard.

'Who is it?' she asked again, rewrapping herself in her sari.

This time the knock was louder and definitely from the sweeper's exit. Hesitant about what she should do, she pressed down the latch and opened the door, just a little. Her first thought was that the sweeper had come late for some reason and that she would immediately instruct him to come later. But before she could say anything, a sprig of fir pushed through the small opening and brushed her face.

Taken aback, she repeated 'Ke?'

'Flowers from A. Chandra,' said a voice, a very familiar voice.

'Flowers?' she was surprised.

A hand came through the little opening of the doors and thrust in an envelope, a slip of delivery that was to be signed by her and a pen, in her hands. On the envelope, in a bold, masculine scrawl, was written her name, a handwriting that was very familiar to her. It was that of her husband! Inside was a beautiful floral card, with a message she would never be able to share with anyone in the family. She blushed. The bouquet had twenty-one pink roses. She was twenty-one years old today and pink was her favourite colour. She signed the slip in a daze and stood frozen inside the bathroom, on the other side of the door, half-dressed, holding onto the beautiful but prickly bouquet, its sweet, fresh scent penetrating her senses.

The man hesitated, and then started to leave. He had expected a tip but seeing her unmoving form, thought otherwise. On his way down he looked up and asked, 'Is there a front entrance to this house? I couldn't find the right door.'

❦

How long she stood in the bathroom like that, she had lost track. She was trapped in a peculiar zone that was in between joy and embarrassment. When someone started pounding on the door, she came back to her senses and realised that she was in a terrible fix. How was she to come out of the bathroom with a bouquet of twenty-one roses and a card that she couldn't allow anyone to read? No, she couldn't face them. They would tease her to death! She couldn't take it. She couldn't let anyone laugh at her husband. It would hurt her.

And what about her father? She felt he would be let down in some way too. And . . . and of course . . . she hadn't even had a bath. . . . !

Night of Illusions

BISHWANATH AND HIS MOTHER TRUDGED UP THE MOSS-COVERED slippery track beside the pond, totally overgrown with water hyacinths. The young man grimaced, carefully avoiding the soft mud on both sides of the trail. His mother, old, but firm, walked with the sure footsteps of one with a mission. Now and then she balanced herself by grabbing her son's arm, forcing him to miss his step. She was fully aware of his unwillingness. He had been dragged into this unpalatable, and in his opinion useless trip to meet some *bhondo* sanyasi.

Now and then, Bishwanath expressed his disgust. It was a Saturday afternoon and his well-deserved half-day had been spoiled, and for what—a remote and totally undeveloped part of Jadavpore, 'outside of civilisation', as he referred to it. The cycle rickshaw had dropped them off at a spot at least half a mile away from their destination. He had said, and rightly so, that beyond that point, the rickshaws did not ply, simply because there were no proper roads. It was a marshy area that had been filled in roughly and allotted to Partition refugees by the government. Desperate for a roof over their heads, many of these hapless families had grabbed what they had come by and fought inhospitable conditions to construct crude huts with their own hands. After decades, some of them had stabilised into one-storey brick houses. Nothing much had changed, though by way of the surrounding ambience.

'There it is!' Bishwanath's mother said with reverence. Bishwanath looked up from his feet, which he had been carefully shielding from the mud, to spot the small, unpainted brick house with a bamboo fence running around it. An old rickety gate with a creaky latch let them into a relatively well-tended garden.

On the tin-roofed porch, *Kapalik* Baba was reclined on an easy chair, his long white beard covering his entire bare chest and navel. A small boy sat on the floor beside him, fanning him with a bamboo hand-fan. Baba's eyes were shut. But Bishwanath's mother went prostrate on the steps of the porch. She always believed Baba had inward eyes.

'Aye,' he welcomed her, without stirring, or opening his eyes.

Bishwanath stood ramrod straight, though his mother nudged him to follow her down onto the rough cement floor.

'Give them something to sit on,' Baba said and the boy ran inside, dropping the fan on the floor.

Bishwanath wondered how long his mother would take. He fantasised about the afternoon nap he had missed. What the hell were they doing here, sitting in front of a man who didn't even bother to open his eyes and acknowledge their presence? But his mother would have some answer to that. She was totally in awe of this Kapalik, who she believed, had great spiritual powers. She had managed to convince all their relatives that everything in her life was due to Baba's *ashirbaad*. Anything favourable that happened in the family was Baba's credit. Anything that went wrong would be blamed on not having consulted Baba or on not having put enough faith in his powers. She was secretly ashamed that the Kapalik probably knew that she had a non-believing son. It had taken a lot of coaxing to bring him here today. He had said that he would accompany her only on one condition, that he would not be drawn into whatever she was going to do there. He had made it clear that he would not have anything to do with the Kapalik. . . . His mother feared his attitude. What if the Kapalik Baba took offence of his statement? He could do anything to anybody by just wishing it to happen.

It was approaching *shondhikhon*—that moment in the evening when day and night meet and remain suspended in twilight. The birds, mostly crows, were creating a racket around them. And a dank smell arose from a stagnating pond, permeating the still air. Not sure where to focus, as Baba's eyes were still shut, Bishwanath turned his gaze towards the trees in the garden. His mother, though, sat cross-legged on the rug placed on the porch, her hands folded on her lap in a posture of total devotion, as if she was attending a puja. Bishwanath sat with his back to Baba, his legs dangling over the steps. His eyes flitted from branch to branch, casually watching the mad rush of sparrows and crows, seeking out their nightly resting places.

'Bishwanath!'

The voice boomed and echoed around the garden. He lurched and wheeled around.

His mother was sitting, just like before, as still as a clay figure, her eyes downcast. The boy had resumed his fanning after laying down the rug for them to sit on. The Baba looked like a yogi in *samaadhi*. None of them seemed to have heard anything.

Bishwanath's brows knitted up slightly and his eyes roved the three faces. But it was obvious that none of them had heard anything. The boy changed his hand, readjusting his posture and continued fanning. He smiled slightly at Bishwanath, who half-reciprocated. A fringe of perspiration broke out on his forehead. He felt claustrophobic, even though he was outdoors.

Just as he was about to turn towards the garden again, something moved in the darkness, behind the door that led into the house. Bishwanath's eyes widened. A very dark young girl peeped out and then vanished into the darkness of the room. The 'jhoom-jhoom' sound of the ankle bells retreating was clearly audible to him. Again, he looked at all the three faces but it was apparent that they had heard nothing. Bishwanath was under the impression, though he didn't know much about the Baba, that he was an ascetic and that he lived alone with only a boy to take care of him. Somewhere inside the house was supposed to be a ten-feet-high Kali *murti*, which he worshipped mostly in private. Only on special nights, he performed *aroti* for his disciples. His mother said this Kali was a living goddess and miracles had been reported by many of his followers.

But this *girl* . . . she had not looked human to Bishwanath. He blinked and chided himself mentally. Yet, he had definitely seen someone or something! Not only the darkness of her skin, which had looked like it had been painted black, but also her eyes . . . he couldn't forget her eyes! They were enormous—the whiteness of the eyeballs almost shining out of the darkness of her skin.

Suddenly, unexpectedly, Kapalik Baba opened his eyes and sat up.

'Time for Ma's *sandhya puja*,' he told the boy. Then, looking directly at Bishwanath he said, almost apologetically, 'My Ma grows restless at twilight.'

Something went haywire in Bishwanath's mind. Did he mean, Ma Kali? How did he know what he had been thinking? He seemed to have answered the question in Bishwanath's mind. Did he mean that the girl had been Kali? Bishwanath's mother looked as unaware as before.

'Do *pranaam* to Baba,' she told him.

Baba's feet were just inches away from where they were sitting. In his confused state, Bishwanath reached out and touched them gingerly. Immediately, the hair on his neck stood up, because now his hands were resting on the feet of a woman—a painted, black feet, with silver anklets around them. He withdrew his hands, as if he had touched fire.

'May you have a long life,' Baba said, rising from his easy chair.

Bishwanath kept staring at his feet. They were slightly swollen and cracked at the heels. They belonged to a very old man.

As darkness descended on the porch, Bishwanath felt an anger swelling up inside him. What gave anyone the right to intrude into his mind? What gave anyone the right to witness his inner feelings, his discomfiture? Restlessly, he walked beside the porch, as his mother continued to sit in her meditative posture, ignoring the clouds of mosquitoes buzzing over her head like a fluid column. Bishwanath swatted them and mumbled a curse under his breath. The boy came out with a lighted hurricane lantern and placed it on the porch. Waiting till the boy had left, Bishwanath walked up to his mother and hissed, 'How long are you going to stay?'

She looked up, hurt. 'If you want to have a cigarette, you can go out and smoke,' she said. 'I can't leave now. He is doing the evening puja.'

But before he could leave the garden, the front door of the house, which had remained shut till then, opened and the towering figure of Kali loomed over them, her wild hair covering her bare shoulders and breasts, and her blood-red tongue hanging out. She held aloft a severed head in one hand and a glinting sword in another. Baba was bent over in front of her figure, offering his obeisance. Bishwanath's mother dived onto the ground face downwards, as if she had been given the most divine privilege in the world. Bishwanath hurriedly folded his hands and touched his forehead.

When Baba rose, he took a brass plate from the floor in front of Kali's feet and held it out towards them. Bishwanath's mother took one *batasha* from it, pressed it to her forehead and put it into her mouth. She gestured to Bishwanath to get his *prasad*. As he approached the plate, Baba himself picked up a batasha and held it before Bishwanath's mouth. It must have warmed the cockles of his mother's heart to see Baba showing such special affection towards her son. Bishwanath somehow felt that the Kapalik knew about his anger and was making a gesture of conciliation. He had no other option but to open his mouth and accept it. But the moment his mouth closed around the humble batasha, he stopped chewing. Instead of the hard brown sugar lump, he felt the softness of a lemon-flavoured *sondesh*, crumbling on his tongue and dissolving. He was scared to swallow. He was even scared to look at the plate. Just then, the boy came in, picked up another batasha and pressing it to his forehead put it into his mouth.

'Today, Ma wanted to have Sandesh,' Baba said, coming from the inner chambers and sat on the wooden separator between the room and the porch. 'She was tired of batashas.'

Bishwanath's mother immediately signalled to her son to offer some money as *dakshina*. Not sure how much was appropriate, he hastily took out the largest note he had in his wallet and passed it on to her. Discreetly, she rolled up the money and placed it on the plate.

'Please offer some sondesh to Ma for her next puja,' she said in a tone of humility.

Bishwanath felt a little dizzy. He had gone without cigarettes for more than two hours now. His mouth felt dry and sweet after the prasad. Unconsciously his hand reached into his side pocket of his kurta and touched the packet of Wills Filter inside.

'*De*. Give me a cigarette,' Baba said, holding out his hand towards Bishwanath.

Bishwanath was speechless. Was he hearing this right? Was this another coincidence? He had never thought that an ascetic like Baba would ask for a cigarette. He had heard of sadhus smoking hookas, but cigarettes?

Baba turned to the boy who had reappeared with the fan.

'Bring that,' he said, indicating something inside the room.

As Bishwanath handed him a cigarette, too shy to smoke one himself in Baba's presence, he noticed the boy placing a human skull beside Baba. He stole a glance at his mother, but she was positioned in a way that she had no view of the side on which Bishwanath was sitting. He felt dizzy and turned pale. He had heard stories of *tantriks* making human sacrifices. But he had always thought they were followers of some extreme cult. But this Kapalik, could this mild-looking old man have practised such horrible things? If not, where did this skull come from?

'*Dhora*,' Baba said, placing the cigarette between his lips and bending slightly forward for Bishwanath to light it for him. His hand shook, as he tried to light the match stick.

Baba dragged at the cigarette a couple of times and then placed it, filter side down, into the mouth of the skull. The bizarreness of the whole scene made Bishwanath feel sick again.

Then, abruptly, Baba turned towards his mother and started enquiring about the whole family. They were in deep conversation when Bishwanath's eyes were drawn to the skull again. Baba hadn't touched the cigarette after those two initial drags. What he saw made him shiver even in the sultriness of the evening. The end of the cigarette lit up and smouldered for a brief moment, as if the skull had puffed it. Then, the smoke poured out of the socket of its nostrils. Bishwanath looked away for some time and then looked back again. He thought he may have been mistaken. Maybe it was an illusion—the play of darkness and dim light. But it happened again. The drawing in of the smoke, the smouldering of the tip and the exhalation of the smoke through the nostrils. . . .

What happened next was unbelievable. This time, the end lit up in two short bursts but nothing came out of the nostrils. 'There,' he thought relieved, 'it was an illusion after all; it was all my imagination! It's all because I'm so bloody tired. I knew I had needed the rest.' But his assurance was short-lived, because, when he looked at Baba, the old man puckered his mouth into a big 'O' and let off a chain of smoke rings into the air above.

Mother and son trudged down the slippery pond-side track, this time in utter darkness. There were no streetlights in this place, and the moon was in *amavashya* phase, only the swinging glow from the hurricane lantern preceded by a long ghostly shadow. Baba had insisted that the boy see them off till the cycle-rickshaw stand.

'You did a good thing by giving him a hundred rupees,' Bishwanath's mother said. 'Anything less would have been inappropriate.'

'A hundred rupees? Who gave hundred rupees?' Bishwanath looked up in surprise towards his mother.

'Then, how much. . . . ?'

'I gave you a fifty-rupee note.'

'But the note you gave me was a hundred rupee one!'

'Ma, I hardly ever carry hundred rupee notes in my wallet. Moreover, it's the end of the month. I couldn't afford to give so much money, anyway.'

For a few minutes a dark silence hovered around them. The chirping of crickets and the swish-swash of their sandals were the only sounds. A firefly darted into the aura of the lamp, lost its glow, and then darted away glowing and gleeful into the darkness beyond.

'Ma Kali Herself gives and takes away,' Bishwanath's mother said quietly. 'Who are we to give Her anything? It's all illusion—all *maya*.'

'That's different,' Bishwanath insisted. 'The fact is that I gave only fifty. . . .'

His mother cut him short.

'You know nothing about what you gave. Neither do you know how much you received in return.'

Bishwanath, taken aback, held his tongue.

The truth of it was that he didn't want to know the truth. He knew that he would never believe what had happened, but it would not be possible for him to forget this night. Again and again, he would hear his name echoing in the garden. He would vividly see the black girl and hear her ankle bells, the taste of the lemon sondesh and the skull puffing his cigarette.

Has Mishtu Eaten Anything Today?

There was a big problem with Mishtu. The plump, comely twenty-one-year-old, who had been a sight for sore eyes, had suddenly stopped eating. Her diet was now restricted to a concoction of lime juice and warm water for breakfast, and endless cups of tea without sugar or milk for the rest of the day. 'Don't want,' was all she said, when any food, however sumptuous, was laid before her. Kalur Ma, the cook who had been with them for twenty years, blamed Mishtu's mother's menu for young Mishtu's sudden aversion to food.

'When I'm bored with cooking the same kind of food everyday, how can she be interested in eating the same food everyday?' she said with unbeatable logic.

In turn, Mishtu's mother blamed Kalur Ma for having lost her magic of preparing tasty food.

Mishtu's father, who equated physical mass with prosperity, started fretting that his fortunes might plunge as Mishtu gradually lost weight.

'It's this new slimming craze,' one of Mishtu's aunts said, 'started by some British model called Twiggy.' She had read this in a women's magazine published in English.

The family doctor whom Mishtu refused to visit, saying she felt fine, recommended some honey to be added to the lime juice-warm water concoction that she had in the morning.

'It will reduce the acidity of the lime and minimise the damage to the lining of the stomach,' he said.

But Mishtu hated the smell of honey. And, in any case, lime in warm water was actually an Ayurvedic cure for acidity, she declared.

Trouble was that it was difficult to argue with an adult. Mishtu seemed to have all the answers, she was well read. In short, she knew what she was doing. More than anything else, this was what scared her mother.

Finally, Mishtu's grandmother thought of a solution—temptation.

'The only way one can make a person break a vow, is by tempting that person,' she said thoughtfully, 'Even muni-rishis fall to temptation.'

'But isn't it true that muni-rishis become muni-rishis because they are able to surmount all temptations?' Mishtu's cousin asked, a little confused.

'Whatever!' Grandma dismissed her, as it sounded too complex.

Her mind made up, she started cooking up her magic. She had been a wizard in the kitchen during her heydays. Now she was semi-retired, due to her arthritis. But, what were minor ailments when she was confronted with the problem of her favourite granddaughter?

Huge *dekchis* full of *rasbadas* and *pantuas* and *pithes* started arriving everyday, with instructions of sending back the dekchi for next day's special feature. The entire family started putting on weight by the end of the month, as they feasted on grandma's delights. Mishtu, of course, didn't touch a single sweet.

Finally, Mishtu's mother asked grandma to stop churning out delicacies.

'You will fall sick,' she told her. 'Moreover, what's the use, she seems to be above all temptations.'

'Has she eaten anything today?'

That was the question everyone was asking, from the neighbours to the relatives, from the cook to the *jamaadaar*.

'Oh-*mago*!' Subala, the maid exclaimed and clucked her tongue in distress. 'It is the same case with the girl at house number 15! She also stopped eating for a year and now she is in wheelchair. Mago! Only if you'd seen the girl in those days—so fair, so healthy, so beautiful she had been!'

None of these concerned remarks, of course, made Mishtu's mother feel any better. Her daughter was slipping away from her, from the world, and she didn't know how to prevent this from getting any worse.

Then one day, Mishtu came home from her teaching job and said, 'I want *thankuni patar rosh.*'

Everyone was dumbfounded.

Why would anyone want to have the juice of pennywort leaves? Only widows craving perverted and bitter tastes to jog their appetites might on occasions have thankuni leaves in soup form. Though kids were often told to have the juice for strengthening their eyesight, very few actually tormented themselves so willingly. But Mishtu's mother and Kalur Ma started making glassfuls of slime-green thankuni patar rosh for Mishtu. At least, it wasn't harmful and at least she had asked for something to eat.

But that was it. Anything else offered edgewise was treated with the same disdainful 'Don't want'.

On certain of her better days, she had a Mary biscuit with her black tea. At wedding dinners, while rows of guests devoured bucketfuls of *luchis*, fried brinjals, vegetable curries, fish curries, meat curries, sweet yoghurt, rasgollas and what not, Mishtu would sit with her banana leaf in front of her, playing with the mound of salt in the corner and dribble the slice of lime all over the leaf. Then, when the chutney appeared, especially the raw mango chutney, she would suddenly sit up and gesture for him to serve some, surprising the person who was serving and disturbing his flow, because he had now adjusted himself to skipping her leaf, after being rejected everytime he raised his ladle to serve her. Then, dipping the crisp papad into the chutney, she would spoon up tiny portions of the sugary syrup and let it drip onto her mouth.

Her mother was sick of all the questions curious people asked her.

'Your daughter isn't eating anything?'

'Is your daughter sick?'

'Your daughter won't have *anything*?'

She wanted to scream and say, 'Yes, yes, my daughter has a serious problem. She doesn't eat and I'm dying from worrying over her.' But of course she never stopped hoping that the old familiar Mishtu would come back, and with her, the healthy girl who had had such a normal appetite. She wanted her back with her fresh, eager attitude to life. She hardly knew this person, to whom no one could talk to; no one could reach out to. She seemed to know too much but kept all she knew, only to herself.

Mishtu's blouses had started to hang down from her shoulders and she had begun to bunch it up at her waist and secure the extra width with a safety pin. Thankfully, the weight loss had not produced any marked effect on her oval face. But, who could ignore those two deep hollows above the collar bone? In Mishtu's case, nobody had ever suspected their existence in her body since she had been so roly-poly since her childhood.

Mishtu had been a success story, before this problem had begun. She had been her parent's pride and joy in every sense of the term. No acquaintance who happened to visit their home, could go through an evening without being forced to see the albums full of Mishtu. The newborn Mishtu in grandma's lap; Mishtu taking her first tottering steps; Mishtu preparing for her first day in school; Mishtu on her fifth birthday, blowing out candles on the cake; Mishtu singing, 'Baa-Baa Black Sheep' in the school concert at ten; Mishtu on horseback in Darjeeling Mall at fifteen; Mishtu in her graduation gown, with one thing common in all those Mishtus—her plump comeliness.

Now, something had happened at twenty-one and like the moon gone behind a cloud, she had become a shadow of her own self. As a result, all those who loved her dearly, were now in a state of anxiety, depression and helplessness.

Her horoscope was read and reread.

'*Shonir dasha*,' the family astrologer said grimly, stretching out the yellow parchment scroll, 'It will make her do strange things, which is not inherent in her.'

He tapped the exact spot in the chart, a box lined in red ink, corresponding to her present age.

'What kind of things?' Mishtu's mother asked fearfully.

'Defiance of authority!'

The old man shot a look over his bifocals.

'Lack of respect for elders!'

He was a shrewd man, quick to gauge her reaction. So he added, 'Other things too, it may negatively affect her health.'

Immediately, he noticed the look of interest in her eyes and the way she exchanged glances with grandmother.

He cleared his throat and adjusted his voice.

'There is nothing that can't be rectified. The onslaught of Saturn can be controlled and deadened by wearing certain stones.'

Mishtu's mother sighed and said, 'It's no use. I can't make her wear anything. She is too headstrong.'

Grandma wasn't a person to give up so easily, though.

'How long will this shonir dasha last?' she asked the man, who was still hopeful of making some extra money out of this.

'Let us see now. . . .' he peered through his bifocals, tracing the chart with his finger.

'Not long,' he said at last. 'Saturn moves away next month, he admitted. And Jupiter takes over . . . but!' Both mother and grandmother looked up, as his eyes peered through his glasses again.

'It always does something vicious before it leaves the house. So beware!'

Beware was said with special dramatic emphasis, sending a shiver down Mishtu's mother's spine. Before leaving, they persuaded the astrologer to offer some pujas to appease shoni. And since such pujas were performed for a price, he accepted the extra money with great detachment.

Meanwhile, the aunt who read foreign magazines that she bought from a second-hand shop near New Market had exciting news for them.

'It's called Anorexia Nervosa. It mostly affects young girls. Apparently, it's a disease that has struck the West and killed quite a few. A young singer with a group called Carpenters died of it. She used to eat nothing but peanut butter in the end,' she reported with a grimace.

Poor Mishtu's mother went down with her own case of 'Nervosa'. She was finding it increasingly difficult to swallow anything, watching her own daughter starve herself.

Grandmother had lived a long, eventful life. She had lived through two World Wars, the Indian Independence Movement, the Partition, Hindu-Muslim riots and at least two famines. She had brought up ten children. And she had survived. But this was a challenge that was unprecedented and she was simply not equipped to deal with it.

'What is it, Mishtu?' she asked, gently, stroking her hair, which, in grandma's eyes had become lacklustre due to lack of nutrition.'You can confide in me. I won't tell *anyone*.'

Mishtu wouldn't have allowed anyone else to touch her hair. But she was too well-behaved to show her irritation to grandma. She went on correcting her school papers, but her body had grown tense. She didn't have anything to say. Not yet. Nothing specific had been asked, yet.

Grandma tucked away a loose strand from her forehead. It made Mishtu feel sleepy. She shut her eyes.

'Are you in love with someone?'

Mishtu opened her eyes, though she didn't look up. Grandma sensed her stillness.

'Who is it?'

Mishtu straightened, pushed her work aside and looked up.

Grandma was smiling, knowingly. Involuntarily, Mishtu's face broke into a reciprocal smile.

'So, you *are* in love!' Grandma was triumphant.

'*Dida*, you are absolutely mad!' Mishtu replied with slight embarrassment.

'I knew it!' Grandma was ecstatic. '*Maadhava, Tuya abhisaaraka laagi . . . Gaagari baari, dharikari peechhala, chalitaha anguli chaapi. . . .*'

Then, answering Mishtu's raised eyebrows, she explained, 'Like Radha says to her lover Krishna, "It is for You, Madhav, that I deliberately pour water on my path and make it slippery, so that I have to press my toes when I walk." You see, love is like a vow. It is difficult to keep. So that when you do realise it, it is all the more sweet. . . .'

'Dida, stop it,' Mishtu laughed, 'I have a lot of corrections to do.'

'I know, I know,' Grandma said, 'I'll go the minute you tell me who it is. I swear I won't tell anyone. It'll be our secret.' Her eyes twinkled with mischief.

Mishtu gave up, 'You know, I'm amazed at you. Where do you get all these crazy ideas? I'm afraid I'll have to disappoint you, because there is no such person in my life.'

There must have been some hint of irritation in her voice, because Grandma stopped smiling. 'If it isn't, then what is it? Why are you doing this to yourself? Has anyone said anything to you? Has anyone hurt you? Whatever it is, you can't go on like this, starving yourself to death. Someday you will be too sick to get up from bed. Then what? Who will look after you after we die?'

The pain and frustration in her voice must have affected Mishtu. 'Arre!' she said, 'Why are you exaggerating so much? Did I ever say that I'll never eat anything again?'

Overcome by emotion, Grandma sat wiping her tears. But she had caught on to a tiny ray of hope . . . something Mishtu had said about it not being a permanent thing.

'You are so bright and clever. What can I say to you? I just hope you know what you are doing.'

She rose to go. 'Just don't hurt your mother anymore, okay?'

As she left, she turned and said, 'Next time I come to visit you, I want to see you eating a proper meal and I'll rejoice in that beautiful sight.'

Mishtu smiled wanly in return.

Before grandma went home, she told Mishtu's mother that there was still hope. Mishtu hadn't gone over the edge. She was confident that sense was going to dawn on her soon and she would begin eating again. According to her, the *temptation theory* wasn't a bad one and she felt it ought to be sustained. She advised Mishtu's mother to keep tempting her with food scattered around the house.

She chided her that the fruit bowl on the sideboard had nothing but bananas in it. 'Put a bunch of grapes there, so it becomes difficult not to pluck one out and put in your mouth when you pass by.'

She peeped into the fridge and expressed disappointment. 'What? No sweetmeats in the fridge?' she exclaimed. 'Who cares for butter and Haringhata milk bottles?'

She sniffed the air inside the house before stepping out.

'No wonder no one has any appetite in this house. It smells like a hospital! For God's sake, this is a Bengali household. Aromas of fish, mutton, ghee and spices should float around, making everyone salivate.'

With these observations and advices, she departed.

But nothing happened for a week. The fruit bowl was now overflowing with grapes. Mishtu's father had bought boxes of assorted pastries from Flury's, which were stacked into the fridge, with strict instructions to everyone else not to touch them. The pantry was stocked with bottles of cashew nuts, pistachios, raisins, specially selected from shops in Burrabazar. The daily menu was overhauled and Kalur Ma laboured over the Galda prawns, which Mishtu used to be fond of. Grandma gladly revived her old arts of making *naroos*, *gojas* and the most difficult and tasty, *narkoler chirey*—finely shredded coconut, just like split rice and coated in fine white sugar. These were attractively displayed in the dining room. But while everyone else's temptation levels were severely tested, Mishtu herself remained stoically above such mortal failings.

On the seventh day, not being able to stand the tension anymore, Mishtu's mother secretly went to meet an old woman. Their maid Subala had contacted this *tuk-tak* woman from her village in the South, known for her magical powers. Apparently, she knew mantras that could bring out the *bhoot*, or evil spirit that may have entered a person. The mission was absolutely covert because of the stigma attached to it. For Mishtu's mother, it was the last resort, though she was ashamed even to admit to herself, that she had stooped so low.

When she returned, well before dinner time, she saw the light in Mishtu's room upstairs and knew that she was in her room, maybe preparing for the next day's lectures. Mishtu's father would still be at the club. And the cook would have left half an hour ago, having made the chapatis for dinner. She had taken the keys with her, so she could slip in quietly and not have to explain where she had gone. But the moment she entered the house, she felt something in the air that made the hair at the back of her neck stand up. Maybe, it was this weird visit she had made. But no . . . The atmosphere inside was full of something she could not define. She heard the muted sound of the radio from Mishtu's room. Exactly as it sounded every evening—the same jangling music of Vividh Bharati, without which she could never concentrate on her work—a peculiar anomaly shared by many young people of that age.

It was the angle of the doors leading to the dining room that first caught her attention. As if someone had rushed in and out through them in a great hurry, and the light in the corridor. That light was never switched on, unless something specific had to be done there. As she came up to the dining room, she stared into it in disbelief.

Kalur Ma always laid the table before she left every night. Even through the gigantic mess she could make out the neatly laid out place mats, the plates and the glasses. This must have happened after she left. Someone had raided the house! There were empty containers everywhere. She could see the bottles in which the dry fruits and nuts had been kept. She checked the cupboards. Yes, they were gone. The pastry boxes lay torn and empty. The steel casserole in which Kalur Ma kept chapatis was empty. The bowl of prawn curry now had only a spoonful of gravy left. She rushed to the fridge and opened it. She stood there gasping. It looked as if it had been mauled by a beast, not a human being. Everything had been ransacked, including the slab of butter. There were even teeth marks on it. The two bottles of Haringhata milk were gone too. Whoever it was, had drank it, unboiled, straight from the bottles and left them on the dining table. The loaf of bread for tomorrow's breakfast—that too was devoured untoasted. Her eyes drifted to the sideboard. The grapes! Each one of the bunch, had disappeared, just the stem lay stripped and bare over a pile of banana skins, a dozen banana skins, to be exact.

Mishtu's mother stood holding onto the back of a chair. A cold suspicion ran down her spine. She knew. Even as she stood staring at the destruction around her, she knew. It was no beast that had raided the larder. But was it?

The sound of retching and gagging penetrated the Muhammad Rafi song. She could hear Mishtu throwing up, but her feet were leaden and just wouldn't move. She stood outside the bathroom feeling like an intruder in a drama, in which she had no role to play. Someone had hijacked her story and now she was doomed to just watch, as it took turns she hadn't intended at all.

The sound of the telephone made her jump.

'Hello, boudi?' It was Mishtu's aunt. 'Have you had dinner, yet? . . . Well, it's late but I thought I'll let you know something I read today . . . It seems, along with the condition I told you about—Anorexia, there is also something called "Bulimia" . . . It says here in this article that this disorder makes a person gorge, and then deliberately purge, either by induced vomiting, or using purgatives . . . I thought you should know that sometimes both the syndromes affect the same person . . . One just can't be too careful, you know? . . . Boudi? Are you there . . . ? Has Mishtu eaten anything today?

Betrayed

MUCH OF OPPO'S FEELINGS FOR HER MOTHER SPRANG FROM THE touch and smell of her skin. On warm, sultry afternoons she would spread her palms on her strong, dark skin and it would be as refreshingly cool as an earthen *kalshi*. On cold winter nights, she would dig her icy toes onto her warm body and instantly feel comfortable. Often, in moments of closeness, she would nuzzle inside the folds of her sari for the soothing fragrance of spring flowers that emanated from her person. She never looked at her mother like others did, as a dark, short, plump and plain woman. She *felt* her mother through her pores and loved her for the feeling of goodness she gave her.

Oppo was often teased for the way she had stood up for her mother when she was hardly four or five years old. Her eyes had flared up, hearing someone describe her mother's complexion as *black*.

'My Mamoni is NOT BLACK!' she had angrily protested, 'My Mamoni is CADBURY CHOCOLATE COLOUR!'

'Of course,' they had hastily agreed, taken aback by her passionate remonstration, 'You're absolutely right,' they had said to pacify her.

Nobody ever mentioned her Mamoni's complexion again, at least, not in her presence.

However, the physical contrast between her parents was often discussed because, unlike her mother, her father was rather dashing and handsome. He had the glint and flash of steel, both in his appearance and temperament and led a life quite far removed from his wife's gentle and homely world. But Oppo had never heard her raise her voice, ever, or complain, even though he often returned home well after midnight from his club. She would always wait for him to make him fresh chapattis for dinner and eat only after he had eaten. Oppo hardly ever got to meet him because by the time he returned, she would be fast asleep and by the time he got up next morning, she would be off to school.

Slowly, as her world expanded, her awareness of her mother became more deeply emotive. She began to sense an immense sadness in her. Even when she smiled, the sadness would roll around her eyes, as if they were in a world of their own. This disturbed Oppo in a strange way. It made her want to protect her from the source of that pain and she felt a growing hatred for whoever caused it.

One Saturday night she woke up with dryness in her throat, in the semi-darkness of the bedroom. She immediately missed the touch of her mother's body and rolling over, found herself in the loneliness of the huge bed that she shared with her. Slipping down to the floor, she squinted at the light outside the doorway and instinctively stumbled towards it in her half-asleep state.

The voices of her parents slowed her down and jolted her awake. It came from her father's bedroom. She couldn't follow the words but it was the tone of her father's voice, like a low, deep snarl that disturbed her. It had hints of something she had never encountered in her ten years of experience, like the ferociousness of a tiger stalking its prey. She immediately shrank and leaned against the solidity of the wall like a frightened child. Then she heard her mother's voice—like a moan, or a sob, with no words. She couldn't gather what was going on but imagined something terrible and incomprehensible happening to her mother. A big, painful lump grew inside her throat and her lips trembled fearfully. Oppo didn't get her drink of water. She curled up on her side of the bed and squeezed her eyes, trying to erase the voices from her mind.

On Sunday morning, Oppo refused to sit next to her father, at the breakfast table. She chose her mother's chair at the far side. Resolutely, she kept her face down, avoiding his eyes. Sunday was family day and the only day of the week Oppo got to meet her father. He would make conversation with Oppo, urging her to eat something he thought was good for her or, ask about her school. In general, he seemed to enjoy being with her at breakfast and lunch on these weekends.

Oppo was a little shy of him and would try to be attentive and well-behaved, like a guest would. She would bask in these little moments when her parents seemed united in their attention and interest towards her well-being. Once or twice she had even made them laugh together at her attempts to use English words she had learnt in school. That they loved her and was proud of her was the unsaid message she was able to comprehend. Most of all, she felt comforted that Mamoni and Babi were 'happy together' with her existence. But somehow last night, the signals had changed for her. She didn't feel like being polite to him anymore.

Her father looked questioningly at her mother, as Oppo seated herself on the far side. Her mother twitched her lips to say she didn't know what was wrong.

'Aparajita, why don't you sit here?' he asked her in a friendly tone. He always addressed her by her full name. After all, he had chosen it himself because she had survived a difficult birth. 'Aparajita' or 'undefeated' he thought was an appropriate name for a fighter for life.

Oppo jerked her head from side to side stubbornly and sat rigid.

'Oppo, Babi is asking you to sit beside him,' her mother said, half requesting, half commanding.

'No! I don't want to sit beside Babi!'

She had almost yelled and the loudness of her own voice surprised her. Her parents stared at her in shocked silence. Oppo had always been a sweet child.

'Let it be,' her father said quietly and started to butter his toast. It was difficult to say whether he was sad or angry.

'Oppo!' her mother called her after she had cleared the table. Oppo, now sullen and morose, replied without enthusiasm.

'Why didn't you sit beside Babi? Why were you so rude?'

'I didn't want to.'

'But why? Do you know how much you have hurt him?'

Oppo was amazed at her mother. Why was she standing up for him? She looked into her eyes and there was the same sadness haunting them. Yet, she was taking his side!

'I hate him! I hate him! I hate him!' she said with vehemence.

And then something hit her left cheek with a smacking sound. Unused to being hit, she looked around her for the source, even as the burning pain induced her left hand to rise and touch the spot. Her mouth agape, she looked at her mother and realised with a slow impact that it was her dear, soft, suffering Mamoni who had slapped her.

'Never, ever, say that again,' she said in a voice so heavy with emotion, that Oppo couldn't believe it was her mother speaking. As her eyes began to blur, her mother said, in a softer and lower tone, 'Your Babi loves you more than anything in his life. You are the centre of his existence. So don't ever hurt him like you did today. Understand?'

The tears now came fast and Oppo cried with the strange broken-hearted wail of a betrayed child. When her mother tried to reach out and touch her head, she moved away with an angry jerk. Now, her mother cried too, because she had never hit Oppo before and her heart ached just as much.

It was difficult for Oppo to sleep that night. For the first time, she lay down on her side of the bed, with a large gap between her mother's and her pillows. She lay facing the wall, curled up in agony.

She heard the sounds of the kitchen die down and the house fell silent. But her mother's side of the bed lay empty. After what seemed an eternity, she heard the soft swish of her mother's sari approaching the door. Oppo turned slowly towards the square of light outside the semi-dark room. She expected her mother to walk in, but only the shadow of her form filled the doorway. Oppo froze herself, pretending she was fast asleep and peeped through her half-shut eyelids. For what seemed a long time, her mother surveyed Oppo's still shape. Then, almost furtively, she tiptoed away towards her father's room. Something made Oppo sit up slowly. Then, slipping down from the bed, she crossed the room and came to the exact spot behind the doorway, from where she had heard the conversation yesterday.

'Are you sure Aparajita is asleep?' her father asked in his low, deep voice.

The conspiratorial sound of her mother's reply sent a shiver down her spine. Her father said something again and this time his voice seemed very different, as if he was begging for something. After a while, she heard a strange panting sound, accompanied by the noise of a creaking bed, which grew louder and faster. Mesmerised, Oppo listened, as her parents moaned like sick animals in various pitches, one moan followed by another, and sometimes overlapping. Then suddenly, her mother's voice rose in a piercing shriek and died away.

Oppo was paralysed. She realised that her throat was so dry that it hurt and her bare feet on the floor felt cold.

Suddenly, very clearly, she heard her father ask, 'What was wrong with Aparajita?'

'God knows,' her mother replied in her gentle, melodious voice but there was an unmistakable ring of laughter in it that Oppo had never heard before. 'Just a bad mood, I guess.'

It was the lightness with which she said it that sent a flash of heat to her head, making her want to hit her mother. Hit, hit, hit her.

An Elegy to 'Boroma'

I used to call her Boroma, a term of respect for older, motherly relatives. But even though I wrack my memory now, I just can't remember exactly what her relationship was with me. She used to live in my maternal grandfather's house—more specifically, in the puja room, on the terrace. I can't recall ever seeing her come down. People came and went in the big house—friends, relatives, and other visitors but Boroma never met anybody. She spent her days, up in the room filled with idols and pictures of gods and goddesses. She made garlands out of the starry *nayantara* flowers, with which my grandmother decorated the idols everyday; she made sandalwood paste by grinding a sandalwood stick with water, on a stone slab. The fused aroma of flowers, sandalwood and the incense sticks burning, is the smell I remember her by. It seemed to have entered the pores of her skin, even her hair smelled of it. The rest of the day, she would sprawl on the cool cement floor and stare into the emptiness, eyes screwed up, nervously pushing a loose tooth back and forth with her tongue. God knows what she used to think about, what she saw in her mind's eye, or whether she thought anything at all.

Because she stayed away from everyone's view, she was never mentioned, or talked about. It was as if, she didn't exist. But every afternoon and night, at lunch and dinnertime, she became the focus of everyone's attention, as my grandmother would try to make her eat, which she would adamantly refuse to do so. Everyone in the family, including our old servant, would make trips to the puja room, trying to coax her, which would end in frustration, till my grandmother scolded, then shouted and then cursed her. Not until she had eaten something, would my grandma eat herself. This distaste for food was probably an early sign of the disease that would eventually kill her, a few years later. Boroma died of liver cancer. For the first time in my life, I saw Boroma leave her abode of the gods to go to the hospital, never to return. She died swiftly, which some said, was a blessing for those who had liver cancer.

Whenever I think of her now, I wonder how many women of her time, wasted away on the fringes of life with nothing to take and nothing to offer. I remember asking my grandmother, why Boroma had this funny hairstyle. It was a cross between a crew cut and a bob, which looked pretty odd in combination with her attire—a white dhoti, worn in the swathed old style and her way of peering into vacant air around her, as if there was something in the transparent space, which only she could see. Now I know, it was because of serious myopia, that she didn't even realise she had. Grandma told me that the odd hairstyle was the result of a cruel, old custom of chopping off women's hair after they were widowed. My grandmother had been lucky. When my grandfather died, she had graduated to a more liberal age of widowhood. She only had to change into white dhotis from coloured saris, take off her jewellery, wipe off her sindur and become a vegetarian. There were many other things, which she was lucky enough to have a choice in, like using soap, or, chewing paan. But Boroma had had no choice. She was only thirteen when her poverty-stricken relatives took her to the burial ground on the bank of the river, in her native place, East Bengal where a mortally ill, fifty-year-old man waited for his call. There, in the briefest of ceremonies, she was married off to him, even as he gasped for breath. It was considered to be a good deed, for which he would be rewarded in heaven, having saved a dowry-less Brahmin girl from the calumny of remaining unmarried for the rest of her life. Luckily for her, the man died almost immediately after the ceremony. Unluckily she became a widow for the rest of her life.

So, this hapless girl, belonging to no one, drifted with the current as the partition of Bengal uprooted her family and somehow she found herself in my grandfather's house in Calcutta. They were distantly related and that was reason enough in those chaotic days to take refuge in anybody's house. But she had also managed to find a space in their hearts and gradually she became an organic part of their large household.

Much later, long after my grandfather passed away, my mother would take me to spend my summer holidays in that house. During these month-long stays, Boroma and I became companions to each other. In the long, sweltering afternoons, when grandma and mother would lie in the relative cool of the darkened, shuttered bedroom, exchanging million stories of domestic life, their voices droning off like drowsy bees, I would explore the vast, quiet emptiness of the huge house, my trail inevitably leading to the terrace. There, I would find Boroma, rolling on the cement floor of the puja room, her dhoti loosely swathed around her otherwise bare body because she never wore any petticoat or blouse, like most of the widowed women of her age did.

I used to spend hours with her, sharing a pursuit other grown-ups found difficult to understand. As Boroma guided me with exclamations, signifying pain or pleasure, I would explore the numerous veins in her body, trying to detect the illusory bugs that she professed, had invaded her veins and were tormenting her. I would hunt for the bugs by tracing my finger along the veins and killing them by the scores. Both of us found a peculiar satisfaction in counting the number of bugs killed, as the hunt continued. When the number reached a hundred, she would ask me if I was tired and say it was enough for the day and that she was feeling much better.

Of course, no one else took the matter of the bugs seriously. It was evident because she never referred to a doctor, to be medically examined. They merely humoured us by going along with it, as they would with any child who was enjoying a harmless pastime. Now, when I think of it, I have this hunch, that maybe the bugs were not totally imaginary. Maybe, they signified some deeper trauma—her unsatisfied longings that were never satisfied, the ones that refused to die with her mythical husband.

I think that my grandmother was the only person, who understood her pain. She never left Boroma's bedside during her last few days in hospital. She was the one, who made the discovery in Boroma's tin suitcase. It was her only earthly possession, besides the few dhotis she wore. As she lay dying, grandma remembered the suitcase and thought it to be appropriate time to open it and see, whether there was something in it that she might like to have before she passed away. What grandma discovered, left her in tears. It contained her red wedding Benarasi, almost disintegrated at the folds, and the mane of beautiful, black hair, that had been lopped off on her wedding day. Both were the only remnants of her few moments of bridehood.

I remember her funeral—the gleam and bristle, as the tongues of fire caught the weave of the silk threads and melted down the gold work and the crackle of the brittle hair, swiftly transforming into ashes. More than anything else, I remember the expression of surreal pleasure on my grandma's face as we stood watching what seemed to be the cremation of a fully-dressed bride. With elation in her voice, she murmured to me, 'At least she didn't die a widow. God took care of that!'

Sonadadu – A Defiant Memory

Sonadadu descended on us once every year, from some remote Indian state, where he served as the Maharaja's personal physician and his hunting companion. I guess it must have been his head full of silver hair, which shone like a crown on his unmitigated black skin, that made him stand out from all others, in my album of memories. Oh, he was pure delight to a boundlessly inquisitive child with an insatiable appetite for stories, jungle stories in particular and Sonadadu never lacked them, having travelled to every jungle area in the world, from Africa to the Amazons. There were numerous sepia-toned photographs of him with the Maharaja, with their legs insolently perched on dead lions and tigers that had been framed and mounted on the walls of our house. The stuffed head and skin of one of his prized Royal Bengal tigers was kept on permanent display in our hall, creating that aura of the forbiddance and mystery that makes every childhood worthwhile.

I still remember the fear with which I would cross the hall at night to go to the bathroom, the yellow glass eyes of the tiger shining through the darkness and the fierce snarl permanently transfixed on the dead face. It's all gone now—the tiger, the photographs, the man himself, Sonadadu died in 1960 and the myth surrounding the man also exploded one day, when I was sixteen.

It all happened in school, one day. A few close friends were showing each other their collections of beads, stones, sea shells and other silly things, which young girls have curious fascination for, when I also happened to show them my cherished memento from Sonadadu. It was the yellowed fang of a tiger that he had given me during one of his yearly visits. What made it particularly dear to me was the fact that Sonadadu had told me, in complete confidence, that he had killed that tiger especially so that he could get its tooth for me.

My friends were so impressed by the story that they decided to show it to our class teacher. Out of sheer natural curiosity, I guess, she picked it up, delicately, with two fingers of her right hand and pressed it down onto the palm of her left, like one would, a precious object. Just as she did so, the tooth crumbled into little pieces, right in front of our horrified young eyes. As we gasped, she exclaimed, 'This is soap stone!'

I've tried to analyse many times why I felt so humiliated, so hurt, so let down that day. Maybe he had never meant it to be a real thing but a token, or a make-believe thing, to stir up the fantasy in a child's hungry mind. But he wasn't around anymore to answer all my questions and restore the boundless admiration I used to have for him. It was as if he had suddenly become ordinary, from the larger-than-life figure I had always made him to be.

I can't remember when the tiger skin and head was removed from our hallway. In fact, the entire house is much changed now and decorated in a lighter, more modern style, without much scope for trapping darkness, or the mysterious. The sepia-toned photographs have vanished too, replaced by bright prints and lithographs. Nothing remains to remind me of Sonadadu. But I do mourn the passing away of that age in my life. Despite all the adult cynicism that has replaced the innocence, the vision of a little black man, with shocking white hair leaps out from some dark corner of my mind and defiantly lingers on.

The Ice Maiden

THE DAY RUNA HAD MISSED HER CLASS AT THE UNIVERSITY TO be with Piltu, she had no clues as to what would happen, only a painfully delicious sense of anticipation and excitement.

Piltu was taking her to his friend's house that he had borrowed for the afternoon, knowing his friend's parents were out of town. After they unlocked the main door with the borrowed keys, Piltu hadn't waited to make small talk. He had gone for her right from the door. The sex had been wild and one-sided. When it was over, Runa wasn't sure of what love meant, anymore. The skin around her mouth felt raw and her body ached. That afternoon she discovered a far different Piltu from the soft-spoken romantic he had appeared to be from the outside. And all the while she had remained passive, almost awestruck by his appetite for her soft, virgin flesh. He had dug into her like a hungry animal, while she tried to show her love for him, by allowing him to do what he wanted. That was the first and the last time. Runa decided she didn't like sex at all. She preferred reading passionate love stories, instead.

Though she often discussed sex with her close friend Soma, who seemed to know everything about the subject, nothing had prepared her for the sweaty and bestial episode with Piltu. Later, at home, she had thrown up every time she remembered the taste of his egg-white semen and the pungent odour of dried urine on his penis. Love or not, she felt that it was vulgar the way he had held his erection with his proud hands and moved it up and down the flat of her stomach and then ejected inside her mouth.

All that seemed ages ago. She had long since moved away from Piltu. His passion scared her. His possessiveness irritated her. His single-minded obsession for her body repelled her. She realised she was content to be unattached. She liked her job as a schoolteacher and to prove her single-minded devotion to her work, did overtime, gave free tuitions and organised special classes for backward students. At night, alone in her spartan room at last, she would lock her door against the world, and lying on her virgin bed with no pillows, and just hard mattress, let herself drift to sleep in the midst of crisp, clean sheets. She liked it that way. Sex in the raw was messy, vulgar and physically distressing.

'Runa, don't tell me you're frigid!' Soma had teased her with cruel candidness, when she heard about the episode later.

Runa's family wondered what had happened to the plump and winsome girl who had once belonged to them; the beautiful child, who could be handled, fondled, petted, squeezed and adored. Though she still lived with them, at twenty-two she had become unapproachable, remote and mysterious—almost ascetic. She made it clear, she didn't like the word *marriage* mentioned in her presence and left the room the moment anyone brought up the topic.

'Perhaps, it is the sexual part that scares you?' an elderly relative had once been bold enough to ask. 'It can be an enjoyable thing, you know,' she had added, knowing fully well that she had broken all norms of traditional adult etiquette.

Runa had immediately thought of the sweaty incident, the swollen lip, the bruised skin, the egg-white. 'Right!' she thought sarcastically, but held her tongue, for obvious reasons. Not for a moment could she let out to her eager family that she had indulged in a love relationship. They were so desperate for any sign of normalcy in her that they might even have forgiven her for an affair with someone they would never approve of. Piltu didn't even come close to being qualified as a suitable match for their prized pet. Runa was meant to be married off royally, to a rich, handsome man, from a good Brahmin family and belonging to an appropriate *gotra* which was very important for a high-caste family like theirs. In their snobbish, snooty perception, Piltu would not only have been disqualified, but also warned off, had they come to know about it.

There had always been an aura of mismatch about their relationship. Runa grew up amidst tall, fair and handsome relatives, but it was the dark, hard masculinity of Piltu's features that had attracted her, as he relentlessly followed her with his intense gaze, whenever they met.

They met one late afternoon, when he was playing cricket on the street opposite Runa's house, while she was watching from her first-floor balcony. He had mistimed a hook shot and raised his eyes to follow the ball's progress as it skied upwards. Their eyes had locked into each other's and in that magnetic moment, the world had fallen away from around them.

Their first kiss had been inside a cabin in Joga's Café, on University Street. It was the most convenient place for them to meet during their university days. Desperate to be with each other, alone, they had stumbled upon this unique place. Inside Joga's Café were the infamous cabins, frequented by broke student-lovers, looking for privacy and cheap refreshments. Joga, a perverted bum, would often catch them in compromising states of necking by entering the cabins without warning. He was a hunchback, who had made a career out of voyeurism.

Their first kiss had initiated their regular lunch-hour visits to the place for almost a year. To their credit, they had succeeded in outsmarting Joga by keeping an eye under the flimsy curtain, where they could see Joga's naked feet, stealthily stalking the desperate lovers in the other cabins.

As Runa snuggled upto Piltu's hard body, he divided his time between devouring his *bresht* cutlet, as Joga pronounced 'breast cutlet', and fondling her breasts. During those early days of their romance, she even loved the smell of his body—a combination of stale sweat, Cuticura talcum powder and a German aftershave his brother had sent him from abroad. The smell of his mouth was that of Wills Filter combined with bresht cutlet, the cheap and expensive mingled to make a unique irresistible brand. In those heady days before the loss of innocence, that smell had only one brand name—love. Runa still remembered that smell and Piltu.

But ever since that afternoon's escapade, she didn't want him anymore. It was as if he had hurt a deep aesthetic nerve within her. However, it hadn't been easy to ward off Piltu's attentions. Everyday, for almost a month, he would wait for her at the bus stop—exactly the way he had done during their year-long courtship.

He was then a college dropout, looking for a job. Runa was doing her masters and preparing for an academic profession. He was street-smart and tough. She was delicate and upper-class. It was a classic magnetism of opposites—pure attraction without verbal communication. Strange, how throughout an entire year, they had met almost everyday, without ever conversing with each other. They would climb to the upper deck of the bus and take the corner of the long rear seat, where hardly anyone noticed them. Throughout the hour-long journey it took them to reach the university, he would sit holding her, his hand cleverly concealed under her sari, their faces giving nothing away, his hands groping her, their minds entwined. After dropping her off, he would return to meet her again for lunch at Joga's Café. Had he not taken her to his friend's house, they would probably have carried on this way forever.

'I can't see you anymore,' Runa said under her breath as he followed her to the bus stop.

'Why?'

'Because my family wouldn't accept you.'

'I'll get a job.'

'That's not the point.'

They were panting because of the brisk walk. She wanted to be as far away from him as possible. He wanted to hold her, touch her body, kiss her and feel his hardness against her soft skin.

'Please don't follow me to the university.'

'That's it? No explanations?'

His face had begun to take on a peculiar flush, an angry purplish tinge, spreading neck upwards through the taut mahogany skin of his clean-shaven cheeks.

'I'll write and tell you what I have to say. . . .'

But a sharp, stinging pain hit her right elbow, as he caught hold of her arm and with one strong jerk, turned her around to face him.

From the corner of her eyes she could see the stares of people, as they jostled each other to get into the bus. They had no time to waste, just enough time to sling those quick, meaningful shots before they disappeared.

'Now, you listen to me,' Piltu hissed and Runa was scared he might explode. 'You might have found it entertaining to have played games with me all this while. . . .'

Runa had somehow managed to extricate herself from his vice-like grip and massaging her elbow, she took her foothold on the bus, as it revved up, vibrated and backfired before moving on. As she adjusted herself to the motion, she heard his last menacing words. . . . 'I'll never let you off so easily!'

It was the longest speech he had ever made and Runa knew instantly, it wouldn't be easy for her.

There were many explanations in the following months. Many written notes handed over and many verbal messages delivered, Soma doing the bearer's job a thankless one, at its best. For months, he would wait for her at unlikely corners; trail her, pounce on her without warning and each time Runa found it easier to just hate him.

Soma pleaded for Piltu.

'If it's your family you're worried about, I can talk to them for you.'

'It's not that. I just don't like him anymore.'

'But why? He's such a nice person! And he's absolutely devoted to you. You don't know how much you're hurting him.'

When all she could elicit from Runa was a stony silence she said, 'He told me he'll commit suicide if you leave him.'

Runa had retorted with scorn and said, 'You seem to be on his side, not mine.'

Soma had tried her best.

'Of course I'm on your side. I'm your best friend. But I do think you're making a mistake. You won't get anyone more devoted or sincere than he is.'

'I don't want anyone. I just want to be left alone.'

Then abruptly, it stopped. Piltu stopped trailing her. Runa had become so used to it that she would sometimes look around her, surprised not to find his silent, accusing presence. She passed her MA and got herself a school job. Her work with children was exhausting, leaving her no time to think of the past. Her family bothered her with marriage proposals now and then, but was gradually learning to accept her independence. She saw less and less of Soma, who was also working now and had become involved with a new set of friends.

Then, one day, she found the envelope in the letter box. It looked like a traditional wedding card in a cream envelope, with the mandatory turmeric mark and an embossed *mangal ghat* in the corner. She was surprised to see it was addressed to her. Her eyes darted impatiently through the antique script and flowery typeface, focusing on the highlighted areas. She locked into the two names that sprung up at her—*Piltu and Soma*. She didn't bother to check the venue or the date.

Night was always a special time for Runa. It was a time she cherished and guarded as her very own, when she was at her lonely best; a time she made love to herself. That night, once she had shut the door, she undressed and got into her thin nightdress. She had a special perfume for bedtime—a touch of jasmine that reminded her of the spiritual love of Radha and Krishna. Next, she went through the ritual of lighting an incense stick that filled her room with the fragrance of sandalwood. She took care to put it in the corner, away from the fan, so the ashes wouldn't scatter all over the floor.

Sensuously, she lifted the bedcover, folded it, and then caressed the soft linen of the bed sheet. Flinging herself on the bed, she began to move her body in waves, to an invisible rhythm. Soon she drifted into her dream world, the plaintive strains of a solitary flute begging her to come to Vrindavan, where her lover waited under a *kadamba* tree.

His dark eyes caressed her face . . . his sensuous lips touched hers and glided down her chin, sending down shivers of ecstasy. The delicate blue vein in her neck throbbed to be kissed. The touch of His playful hands on her aroused nipples sent quivers down her navel. As her body exploded with desire, she screamed for more.

Surrounded by the maddening, deafening, teasing strains of the flute, her body moved and fell in perfect synchronisation with the presence that filled her body, and they merged into each other, body and soul. . . .

'Don't stop,' she begged in her silent room.

'Don't stop,' she begged in her virgin bed.

'Never,' her love whispered, '. . . now we shall be together, forever. . . .'

The Piano

PARIMAL ROY GENTLY PUT DOWN THE CAR KEYS ON THE sideboard and glanced towards the door of the next room. From inside, the strains of Mendelsohnn's Opus 5 on violin drifted plaintively from under the door and mingled with the sadness in his heart. Very soon, his only daughter Anisha, who was blissfully playing violin in her room, would leave her childhood home and become someone's wife. He would miss the sound of her music, which filled the house all the time. Anisha was crazy about Western Classical, a passion he shared with her. Then, remembering something, he smiled and the tiredness on his ageing face, somewhat lessened.

'Good news?' He hadn't noticed his wife coming into the room. She studied his face, as she wiped her turmeric-stained fingers on a towel and straightened the end of her sari, which was crushed from being tucked at her waist. She knew from thirty years' experience that there was something hopeful in his eyes.

'Tea?' she asked and without waiting for his answer, walked away to the kitchen.

'At last, I think, Ani won't mind getting married,' he said, following her.

'Why, have you found her a piano for a husband?'

There was a mixture of sadness and mockery in her voice.

Then, she added thoughtfully, 'If they don't ask for dowry, you can easily buy her a piano.'

'They have asked for dowry. But they also *have* a piano!' he said, half triumphantly, half regretfully.

The kettle had started to whistle but she had forgotten all about the tea. Hurriedly, she moved back into the drawing room, pushing the end of her sari back into her waist. 'How much did they ask for? Did you see the piano? Did you tell them that Ani plays the piano, the violin and the guitar?'

Parimal Roy suddenly felt stupid in the heat of her enthusiasm. He reminded her of the boiling kettle. While she noisily washed the cups and measured out the tea leaves, he quickly went through the details in his mind. He admitted to himself that he hadn't been thinking practically. He had actually had no discussions regarding the piano or, Ani's musical nature. The moment he had met the prospective bridegroom's father, he had disliked the fellow. Straightaway, after the introductions were over and they had seen Anisha's photograph, the man had broached the subject of dowry, in a subtle way, of course, because the word itself had become taboo in Bengali society. But Parimal Roy had clearly understood the cryptic language, with references to furniture, gold, household items as well as cash.

It was only when he was leaving the house that he had happened to catch a glimpse of the polished and gleaming four-legged furniture, at the far end of the room. In his mind, he had been trying to find one good reason why his educated and talented daughter should marry into this pompous, dowry-seeking family, when he had seen it. A piano! Why, Ani had always had her heart set on one, ever since she had learnt to play it. He had even enquired around for a second-hand one. But pianos were so rare nowadays in the city. And a new one would be terribly expensive.

The sound of the violin had stopped in the other room. As Mrs Roy laid out the tea tray, the door opened.

'Baba, you're home!'

Before he could reply, his wife babbled out the surprise. 'Finally, you've got what you wanted,' she said with enthusiasm. 'You will be able to play your Beethoven, Bach and Tchaikovsky. . . .'

Anisha looked from one face to the other. She knew her father had gone to visit some prospective groom's house. She never kept track because she wasn't interested. All she cared about was her music. It was her dream to own a piano.

'You've bought me a piano?' she asked, incredulously.

Parimal and his wife looked at each other. Then, gently, her mother said, 'Now we leave it to you, Ani. There is a rich family, who owns a piano. We know how you feel about this dowry thing, but where else will you get a piano? Of course, we won't force you into anything. Just think it over, Ani . . . your dream may come true!'

'How could an intelligent, educated girl like you do this? We have always sworn to each other that we would never marry anyone who asks for dowry!'

Anisha seemed suddenly to have grown up. It was partly due to the lot of thinking she had done, before saying yes. The easy part had been the piano. The hard part was the dowry. She had weighed each against the other, carefully. There wouldn't have been a doubt had there been no piano.

'You have to do certain things for your parents,' she told her best friend.

'Nonsense!'

She needed more to be convinced by. They had been through school together and she knew Anisha wouldn't think of doing something so against their strongest beliefs, just because she loved her parents.

'You're marrying for the piano, aren't you?'

Anisha remained silent.

'God, how stupid can one get! You're sacrificing your life and happiness for the sake of a silly piano?'

Suddenly, Anisha looked straight at her friend's animated face.

'My life and my happiness is the piano. That's the difference between you and me.'

She got up and left. Stunned and confused, her friend continued to sit, trying to figure out what she really meant.

Only one shining dream had taken Anisha through the madness of the last few days. First, she had lost her pride and her best friend. Then, she had lost her home where she had lived the first twenty-one years of her life, to go to live at someone else's place. Last night, after the guests had gone away and she and her husband were pushed and locked into their bedroom by giggling women relatives of all ages, she had lost her virginity on a king-size bed strewn with rose petals. She hadn't slept a wink after the painful experience, as she watched the snoring stranger beside her and dreamed of the piano. She had had enough, she told herself. She had earned her right to use it. She was determined to ask him for it now. . . .

'What is it? What is it?' everyone asked.

The house was still full of relatives who had come to attend the wedding from other cities. They had been awakened by the sound of her screams and wails. Now they gathered outside the bedroom door, half asleep, half curious, half alarmed and some wiser than the others, half amused.

'Maybe, we shouldn't interfere. Maybe, she was just scared by the whole thing,' they said. But the door was pushed open and Anisha charged out of the room, dragging her dazed-looking husband behind her, as they were still attached to each other by their sacred scarves. Tears streamed down her face, messing up her stale make-up and all they could hear through her sobbing was, 'It can't be true . . . my father saw it with his own eyes. . . .'

As she walked up and down the rooms, with the entire shocked family following her, trying to calm her, the bridegroom pleaded with everyone, 'Someone please tell her . . . we don't have a piano . . . her father must have seen the old teakwood bureau in the drawing room. . . .'

Buro Ma

SHE HAD NO NAMES BUT WAS UNIVERSALLY KNOWN AS BURO ma, or, Old Mother.

Half-blinded by cataract, she was like a seventy-two-year-old monolith, towards whom the family gravitated—Dr Ganguly, his wife, his two daughters, the servants, and an army of relatives and friends.

She squinted and puckered her toothless mouth, letting out the choicest curses, as her two young granddaughters giggled in merriment. The targets of those curses were the handful of policemen, who were patrolling outside their garden gate.

'*Ki*, Buro ma, your son not home for lunch?' they called out from outside the garden wall.

They had obviously not spotted the black Austin of England, parked inside the garage.

'Burnt-faced monkeys!' Buro ma returned, seated like a granite sentry on the small balcony overlooking the garden.

'Have they heard me?' she asked the girls, who were hiding behind the door, to confirm.

'Fat-headed pigs! Haven't you seen the car in the garage? And how dare you make so much noise with your boots. Mosh-mosh! Mosh-mosh! Can't a hard-working doctor take a well-earned nap? If you wake him up now, I'll kill you all, sons of prostitutes!'

The policemen laughed.

'Okay, okay, let him sleep. We can wait.'

'Sons of pigs, sons of whores, sons of . . .' she kept on grumbling, but did not budge from her sentry position on the balcony. The two girls were her eyes. From behind the door, they continuously reported on the whereabouts of the policemen.

In actuality, Dr Ganguly was far away from home. At that very moment, he was at a secret venue. He had gone there to warn them that the police had got wind of their activities. He suspected that they were closing in on him. They were not absolutely sure yet, about his role in the vast network of anti-British enterprise and were just trying to keep a very close eye on his whereabouts. The moment they found something concrete, they would raid his house. Dr Ganguly being a very well-known surgeon in the city, they were exercising extreme caution.

The doctor's plan to confuse the police had been meticulously worked out. When he was going on any revolutionary work, he slipped out from the backdoor exit, keeping the car in the garage. This was meant to keep the police off his trail. The rest was done by Buro ma. She sat in the balcony and cursed the uniformed men, off their backs. In fact, her verbal lashing was so effective that the police stopped their marching and ultimately left, assured that the doctor was at home and not out on any anti-government work.

The other part of the plan was to send them off on a wild goose chase. When Dr Ganguly was actually at home, his garage would be empty. This was achieved by leaving his car somewhere else, on his way from work, and then returning home by the back door.

'The stupid cows are back grazing the fields again,' Buro ma would mock them. 'The donkeys don't even check the garage to see he's out. They think the entire day my son only sleeps. *Arre*, my son is an important doctor! He has no time to rest.'

'*Jah-jah*!' she would dismiss them with her hands, '*Hath-hath*!' then clap her hands, as if she was shooing away cows from her fields.

To their credit, the policemen never took offense at the way they were treated by the eccentric lady. That a sane lady, however old, would curse them the way she did, was beyond their comprehension. But they just laughed and joked with Buro ma. Dr Ganguly couldn't have chosen a better foil for his purpose. In fact, her play-acting was so convincing, the police temporarily stopped the trailing. They probably reported to the authorities that their tracks had run cold, maybe to protect, what they believed, was the family of a hard-working Bengali doctor and his old, eccentric mother. They could not believe that such a family could be involved with terrorism.

They, of course knew nothing of Buro ma. They had no idea that it wasn't eccentricity but pure spunk that characterised and drove this remarkable woman. People outside Ganguly's immediate family had absolutely no idea that she was not doctor's natural mother. Her past was as extraordinary as a fairy tale with hair-raising circumstances. As a child, she had survived the most impossible of all odds and challenges like these were no match for her.

Legend has it that Buro ma came from a village, far from the city of Calcutta. She was the sole survivor of that village, which was wiped out by an epidemic of cholera. Legend also says, that on a cataclysmic night, some sixty years ago, when a raging cyclone swept over the dead community, the single survivor, a twelve-year-old girl, spent the night lying face downward, pressing on the dead bodies of her mother and sister, till the first light of dawn arrived and the storm had transformed into a torrential downpour. Then, she on her weak childish feet, tottered out of the gutted hut. With nothing on her person but the flimsy cotton rag swathed around her body she began the long walk that brought her to the big city of Calcutta.

But it wasn't till twenty years later, that she came to the Ganguly family, accompanied by a well-wisher. She was then a worldly-wise thirty-two-year-old woman, having worked in a number of houses. The cook at her previous workplace had been making lewd advances and she had escaped with another maid servant's help. She had been told that this family wa kind, large-hearted and well-to-do and would definitely have a place for her. This was an encounter that changed her whole life around.

When she recalled that fateful day years later, there was divine trance on her face. She narrated how she had stood at the bottom of the staircase, looking up at the mesmerising scene.

'Ma Bhabani came down the staircase, holding her baby in her arms . . . She had just bathed and her wet black hair fell around her face and neck like monsoon clouds . . . some of her jet black hair clung to her naked white shoulders in sharp contrast to her skin gleaming like gold . . . and her moon-shaped face radiating divine peace and love. . . .

'*Ney*,' she said, looking down on me and holding out her baby. '*Tor chheleke dhor*'. It was as if she was waiting for me. It was as if she was passing on a sacred burden to me.'

All this, she narrated to the children of Dr Bishweshwar Ganguly who listened to the story, open-mouthed from their grandmother—Buro ma. They had only known one grandmother and had been taught to love and respect her. Their real grandmother had died years ago and had been lionised as the family saint by all those who had known her. She had passed on her baby to this unknown woman and devoted herself to meditation and spiritual guidance after her husband died following the baby's birth.

The day Buro ma entered the gates of this house, the day she held the beautiful baby boy in her arms and felt connected to him as deeply as a mother would, she lost all memory of her past. Gradually, over the years, she came to be referred to as *Bishur ma*. Nobody doubted her devotion. Nobody questioned her authority. Such was the power of the occurrence that though she was penniless, illiterate and plain, she was accepted as part of a divine process.

Bishu grew up under the jealous motherhood of his adoptive mother and the benevolent guardianship of his two uncles and their wives. He made them all proud by his academic achievements. Every time an exam was near, Bishur ma would go to the puja room and touching the feet of 'Ma Bhabani', inform her about it. It was her firm belief that Bishu's achievements were due to the blessings of this divine lady. She lived till Bishu became a doctor. And then, one day, as if to mark the end of her life's mission, she declared that it was time for her to join her husband in heaven. She died, smiling in her sleep, leaving no doubt in anyone's mind that she had indeed, done so.

Now, only she, Bishu's 'Buro ma' was left to be his guardian angel. Though Dr Ganguly's wife was chosen and approved of by Buro ma personally, she was exceedingly jealous of her daughter-in-law. She was scared that this beautiful, cultured girl would steal her son's heart from her. Knowing her feelings, both the doctor and his wife were careful to give her their prime attention. Often, to get his full attention, Buro ma would fake illness and then the doctor would rush home and find her in bed.

'Ki, Buro ma, how are you feeling?' he would ask her with concern.

That was what pleased her the most, giving her a sense of victory over her daughter-in-law. She would then pour out all her complaints against his wife, his two daughters, the servants and the entire world at large. The doctor would listen patiently as she would go on describing all sorts of undetectable pains in her body, though she was really as strong as an ox. After checking her heartbeats with his stethoscope and examining with his torch, he would give her some innocuous potion, just so she felt loved and cared for.

But Buro ma would not be remembered for her weaker moments. What made her so remarkable though, was her tremendous courage. During the fearful days of the Hindu-Muslim riots, when even a distant call of *Allahu Akhbar* would be enough to send shivers down the spine of all Hindus, she would stand on the open terrace, boiling oil in an iron pot upon a mud oven, to be poured on Muslim rioters, if they tried to raid the house. These were days of extreme violence, when bands of Hindus and Muslims raided each others' areas, killing indiscriminately. No woman even dared to come out of their houses. But Buro ma organised all sorts of protective measures and kept everyone's spirits with constant rousing exhortations.

'Let them come,' she would declare, 'I will see to it that none of the bastards go back with their tools between their legs!' And no one had any doubts in their minds that she would carry out exactly what she threatened to do. All sorts of gadgets and tools were sharpened and kept ready at her bidding.

It was probably her early experience of utter tragedy and deprivation that had given her the edge of steel and the hardness of metal. Like all courageous people, she was driven by a singular devotion—her Bishu, the son God had entrusted to her care. Nobody could take him away from her, let alone harm him in any way, least of all, the sycophant policemen who 'licked the boots of their English masters', in Buro ma's words.

But they came alright, one day, for Dr Ganguly, whose name they had finally found in some scrap of paper, that another activist had failed to destroy. It was one of those days, when the Austin of England was parked in a friend's place and the doctor was home. They came with a warrant and this time, without the smiles and jokes. As the servants argued and stalled at the gate, the doctor hastily dressed, having been woken up by the family. A plan was quickly made in hushed whispers. Buro ma would try and convince them that he wasn't home, while he would escape from the back door. The time had come, he said grimly, to carry on the movement from underground. It would have worked, too. He was ready to depart, when the argument between the inspector and Buro ma flared up. She said that her son wasn't home. He said that he had a warrant to search the place and he would. She said, 'Over my dead body,' and the brave old woman spread her hands, barring the path of the inspector. Grimly, the inspector said he would have to do his duty and requested her not to force him to do anything he didn't want to do. Buro ma dared him. Within a split second, just as the doctor was about to depart, he heard the screams of the servants and the sound of someone falling. In a flash, the doctor turned and rushed back in.

They arrested him, even as Buro ma lay unconscious on the floor near the hall entrance.

Waiting to Go Home

'GO CAREFULLY,' BONDONA'S MOTHER SAID ANXIOUSLY, following her to the door.

'Times are bad,' she added grimly, as if her saying so would reduce some of the danger that she imagined.

Bondona fussed with the fall of her sari. She wore it slightly higher than most girls of her age, and tucked its loose end onto her waist to keep her hands free. It was a kind of deliberate attempt to look and feel 'matter-of-fact'– even a trifle drab. She needed people to understand that she was serious about her studies and that she wasn't in it for flippant reasons, like keeping herself occupied till marriage or having some fun with the boys in the university.

In reality, the journey from Ballygunge Station to College Street by the No. 2 bus demanded full physical preparedness. It was good that her mother didn't have the faintest idea of how she travelled each day. Bondona didn't want her to know. As it was, she worried every moment her daughter was away from home. Even late last night, erratic sounds of bombs exploding on the *kasba* side of the railway track had kept her awake. Isolated reporting of stabbings and burning of trams and buses were there in the papers almost everyday. In fact, she didn't know many other things because, if she did, she would have worried herself sick. The Naxalite movement had created a vague atmosphere of unrest that barely touched the lives of people like them, except at the fringes, like when there were incidents of disruption of the city's transport system, now and then. Or, when, occasionally, in the areas adjoining Ballygunge Station, people would hear a succession of explosions and the vibes would spread by mouth about some *maramari* between rival political groups. Rickshawallas would refuse to go to those areas after dark. In the lanes around these areas, the doors and windows would immediately be bolted and it wasn't unusual to see young men running like flashes between houses, their faces dark with intent and their hair wild. The local doctors got many cases of torn and bloodied limbs brought in by men who posed fiercely around their clinics, snatching up the victims as soon as they were patched up, and vanishing into the night without paying even a penny. Those doctors had learned to keep their mouths shut afterwards.

For Bondona it was an advantage that her mother was absolutely homebound and a typical Bengali housewife, whose days' work never seemed to end. Before being posted out of Calcutta, her father had always escorted her to wherever she had to go. She didn't know much about trams and buses to venture out on her own. So now that he wasn't around, she felt a little helpless.

'Offo . . . o . . . o!' Bondona retorted to her mother's words of caution, glaring at her irritably.

Her mother wiped her wet hands with the end of her sari and watched her daughter go off into the unsafe world outside. She still thought of Bondona as her little girl. Only now, instead of playing an active role in getting her ready, she was destined to watch. During the early schooldays she used to take pride in dressing her up in her spotless uniform, washed and ironed by her personally. The short, blunt-cut hair neatly parted at the centre and forced into two little pigtails that stuck out on both sides of her round face in a mischievous glee. Even the red ribbon bows were perfectly matched, with the knots at the centres, of the same size. She would polish the shoes on the previous night and keep them ready, shining and propped-up against the wall like two little boats. According to her, those were the best, most perfect days, and she fondly dusted the photograph her father had taken one of those days, before she left for school. Sadly now, she glanced at the rubber band twisted with impatience around a hastily-made ponytail. Carelessness about her appearance had seemed to become a statement with Bondona. The focus had shifted to the heavily-laden shoulder bag. Her only contribution to the daily expedition was the small bottle of XXX Rum filled with water, boiled and strained for drinking. All her attempts to pack her a lunch had failed, however.

'Are you crazy? Do you think travelling by bus is like going on a picnic? It'll get totally squashed! I don't want food on my books and papers.' In actuality, more than the inconvenience, it was the sense of restriction in the small tiffin box and the stigma attached to it in the campus that made her say that. Along with the lack of rules, it was the aura of casualness that was attractive about university life. Girls and boys who had, only a couple of years ago, opened their lunch-boxes with clockwork regularity at *tiffin time* and gulped down cold and soggy sandwiches or luchis, now rolled up in noisy groups around pavement *puchkawallas*. As the man did his incredible act of squashing a hole in the crisp puchkas, packing in the potato filling and immersing them for a brief moment in the pitcher of tangy tamarind water, all in one swift, continuous motion, the salivating students would be busy positioning themselves around him so that their clothes would be out of range of the leaking puchkas handed out in a splashy jab of motion. They were adept at plunging the rounds into their mouths and gulp and chew at the same time and be ready for the next helping within seconds. Bondona had realised early enough that one needed special skills and a lot of practice to participate in these puchka rituals. At first she couldn't even open her mouth wide enough, nor could she gulp and chew and be ready for her next helping so fast. But gradually, even she had got into the rhythm and wasn't shy to open her mouth wide. She had been stupid enough to let slip to her mother one day, about these roadside rituals and regretted it.

'Do you know *how* they make these puchkas?' she said aghast. 'Do you know that they blow their noses and then make the puchkas with the same hands?'

But it was useless. She stopped trying. All she prayed for now was to get through this unhappy patch in life. With her husband away and her daughter growing more and more rebellious day by day, she desperately wanted him to return quickly and take this responsibility back into his hands. She wanted Bondona to pass out as soon as possible. And she wanted her father to find a good match for her. She didn't want to be left alone in the house, worrying all by herself.

'Durga, Durga,' she prayed intently, as Bondona eased into her Bata sandals and pulled up the straps into the grooves above her heels. As she left, she raised her hand slightly, to indicate she was off.

She didn't mean to be unkind to her mother but she did want her to know that she could take care of herself. Ever since her father's departure, she had taken the opportunity to assert her independence. Part of this moving away was to do everything her peers did, to bathe in the common life, to feel in-tune with the city she had grown up in and expose herself to its unpredictability and dangers.

Her father had been extremely critical when she had told him of her intentions of doing her MA from the Calcutta University. According to him, Jadavpur University was good enough. It was closer to home and safer—not plagued by students' unions and protests and things like that. Also, his mind was full of the kinds of things that happened in public buses. The lecherous bastards doing unimaginable things to women in the crush of bodies during rush hours, was distasteful for him to even visualise and anyone doing the same to his daughter, whom he had brought up sheltered from the big bad world outside was simply unimaginable.

In fact, Bondona's college mates had teased her mercilessly for being chaperoned to and from the college everyday. For most college girls relative freedom began with college life. It was an unmarked boundary line beyond which most of the 70s girls were allowed to bend a few rules they were once strictly enforced during their schooldays, like going to adult movies with friends, or staying out late or having non-serious boyfriends, whom they addressed as *dada*, if they were older, or as *tui*, if they were of the same age, so as to deliberately confuse the sexual nature of the relationships. Bondona had been envious of the ease with which her college mates obtained permission for spending time with their friends. She often got angry when she was told she couldn't go. She found it humiliating and often, embarrassing, that her friends had to come to her home and persuade her parents to allow her to go to a movie with them.

'*Mashima*, I'll look after her. Don't worry.'

'*Meshomashai*, we'll make sure she reaches home by six.'

Why was she condemned to have such strict parents? 'Why couldn't they be a bit more normal?' she used to think wistfully.

But now that things had changed with her father having gone out of Calcutta, she intended to take full advantage of her situation. Her father had had no choice but to sign the application form that she brought. Bondona was a little surprised, as she had anticipated a tough fight. She had been ready with her tears, her outburst. But nothing like that happened. It was probably because he knew he would not be able to exercise any hold over her now that he would not be physically present.

After leaving her house, Bondona turned that corner of the road from where she couldn't be seen anymore by her mother, who she knew was still standing at the gate watching her disappearing out of her sight. Often, her vegetable curry would get slightly scalded at the bottom, or the *machher jhol* would reduce too much, but she had to watch Bondona till the last glimpse, for her own peace of mind.

There had been a buzz going around in the corridors of the Calcutta University the day before, that there would be a student union strike. This normally meant no classes. The professor would return to his office, not being allowed to enter the classroom. And the students would go off gallivanting, not even bothering to come to class. For Bondona it meant she would have some extra time to spend at the library. The lectures were anyway boring and quite useless. The students had no illusions about learning anything special from them. They kept themselves focused on the exam that was two years away and made notes from the reference books that were suggested during the lectures. Those who attended classes regularly, did so to keep their attendance percentage, or, because they were used to the ritual of entering a classroom everyday since childhood. It was very usual for the students to give *proxy*, which meant answering to someone else's name during the roll-call. It was a favour students exchanged with each other. Such things were systematically overlooked by the administration. They probably had bigger headaches to handle. Bondona was fascinated by these cultures and it made her feel grown-up to be a part of them.

Knowing that there would be no classes, Bondona decided to look up some reference books at the small USIS Reading Room off the College Street. It wasn't that she wouldn't find what she needed, in the University Library. But using as many libraries as possible was part of the process of widening the university experience. It had a nice ring to it too. 'I went to do some reference work at the USIS sounded important. In fact, most students used all the libraries in the city, including the British Council on Theatre Road, the National Library in Alipore, as well as the Ramakrishna Mission Institute Library in Gol Park. Memberships in these libraries meant that you were *into it*. Moreover, they gave students an extra excuse to spend time away from home.

Bondona walked down College Street, towards the congested crossroad area, where she turned right. It was housed on the second floor of an old commercial building. The moment she went up the narrow staircase to the carpeted reception area, though, it seemed she had entered a different planet. The cool air from the air-conditioned reading room greeted her in short welcome blasts, as the students passed in and out. The total silence inside, punctuated by the crisp sounds of turning pages, created an aura of being in a quiet, brisk enterprise.

She selected her book and chose her place which wasn't too close to any other reader. After her long walk in the heat and noise outside, she felt that she was dozing off in the silence and comfort. She was hardly through a single page when the sound of someone snapping his fingers brought her out of her paradise. In any other place she wouldn't have bothered to even look up. But in this reading room the sharp staccato sound cut into her senses. She lifted her head and turned towards the long aisle which spanned the two exits on opposite sides of the room. By then, all the readers were staring amazed at a lanky, dishevelled young man walking down towards the inner exit way, snapping his fingers, as if to an internal rhythm. Just as the man reached the door on the far side, to a cue, all hell broke loose.

Suddenly, the long, polished tables near the shelved walls came alive. Readers who had appeared to be in deep study, jumped up from their seats like programmed robots and began lifting the heavy leather-bound books from the shelves and pitching them at random, towards the centre of the room. The screams began just as some of them found their targets. In the stampede that followed, men, women, books, journals, papers, spectacles, bags, shoes, and sandals crashed into each other from all directions. The small glass-paned swing door towards the exit was wrenched from its hinges and splinters of glass were smashed into smithereens under the press of feet, the crunching sound adding to the high-pitched wail of the fleeing crowd.

Bondona had begun to move with the first rush, some primal urge dictating her to just run for her life. She did not have a single thought other than a hell-bent desire to escape. From the landing down the staircase, she lost her foothold and was simply carried down by the swell of bodies, as she managed to hold onto her shoulder bag for dear life. At the base of the staircase, she found the ground again, as the bodies spilled out through the gate into the bright sunlight of the pavement. People outside had started to crowd around, watching the spectacle of the frenzied outpouring. Nobody knew what was happening inside or what kind of help was needed.

All at once, Bondona found herself in the familiar world of heat and congestion of the streets. Trams, buses, fruit sellers, bookshops, sweet shops, sari shops and hundreds of unconcerned people, driven by purposes of their own, yet managing to crisscross the streets without intruding into each others' spaces. And for the first time in her life, she felt thankful for it. At the corner of the street, where it joined College Street, she stood and breathed deeply, to calm her fast pounding heart. Only then did she realise that she had been scared out of her wits. But now, assailed by the heat and noise around her, a feeling of reassurance crept in. It was hardly a few hundred steps away from where she had escaped intact, yet the vibes of the happening had not created a single ripple here. It was as if nothing at all had occurred and the whole thing had been a bad dream from which she had just woken up.

The sun was bouncing off every surface and Bondona felt she needed her sunglasses. As she plunged her hand into her bag to retrieve them, she felt a sharp, stinging pain on her right shin. When she tried to feel the place through her sari, certain wetness there told her that it was a bleeding wound. Strange, she couldn't even remember being hit by anything. But it was difficult to remember anything clearly about those few hellish minutes inside.

A rhythmic sound pounded her ears. . . . Turning towards the building she had left a few moments ago, she could make out the all too familiar sight of fists being raised in unison to what she imagined would be some anti-American slogan. The trouble-makers must have completed their job inside and had come out and surrounded the place to make their verbal protests. She could already see some policemen moving around warily. Bondona didn't want to be in this place anymore. It made her nervous. She quickly summoned a rickshaw passing by and with difficulty, climbed onto it. Her leg had started to throb.

'Where?' the rickshawalla asked, before lifting it up.

'University bus stop,' she said, hurriedly.

Now she wanted to return home as soon as possible. It would be easier to get into a No. 2 now, being lunchtime. Suddenly, she remembered her mother's caution in the morning

'Go carefully,' she had said. To Bondona it seemed morning had been a lifetime ago.

Her mother would be surprised to see her home so early. She would come down half sleepily, half anxiously, from her bedroom upstairs, to open the door. It would be cool inside the house now, especially the ground floor. Bondona loved to walk barefoot on the red cement of the flooring. The rooms had black and white geometric patterned tiles. Often, during summer afternoons her mother would wet a bamboo mat and lie on the floor. All the green-shuttered windows would be shut against the hot air outside, only a muted light coming in through the balcony door where the laundry, almost dry, would keep the glare out. There would be a *Desh* magazine lying open and upturned beside her pillow. She could never complete a story—always falling asleep before she reached the end of the first page.

Bondona held her leg as the rickshaw rattled over the tramline, making it hurt. She could already see the bus stop down ahead, strangely deserted at this hour. It was perhaps because of the university strike. She couldn't tell her mother about the strike though, nor about the USIS episode.

A No. 2-bus blasted past her rickshaw, as the puller swerved out of its way, cursing. It took more effort to pull over the tracks because of the grooves. Bondona watched helplessly as the bus screeched to a halt for just a few seconds to let a passenger out and roared away from the empty stand. They were just a little too far behind. On an ordinary day she would have stopped the rickshaw, paid him hurriedly, and sprinted for the footboard. But now her leg was aching badly. She would have to wait at least another half hour for the next bus.

All of a sudden, she felt weary, hungry and homesick. For a second she remembered the taste of rice and liver curry. She knew her mother had cooked liver today. It was her favourite. Though she never went home for lunch, for some odd reason her mother always kept some lunch aside for her. Then, every night she would have her lunch and dinner together.

Leaving the rickshaw, she leaned against the railing of the bus stop shelter, so she wouldn't hurt her leg. Pain was something that invariably turned her mind homewards. She would have to lie about the wound. Scraped it in the bus, banged against a table, cut by a rickshaw; I'll make up something in the bus, she thought. Her mother would be concerned that she had gone without first aid for so long. 'The streets are so dirty and full of germs!' she would worry and call '*Dactarbabu*! It could become septic,' she would say.

'No, no,' Bondona decided, she wouldn't tell Ma anything. It would vindicate her anxiety for her. She could always clean the wound herself and then apply Boroline or something.

If only the bus would come soon.

Opposite to the bus stand, the gate of the university wore a totally deserted look. The entire area looked forlorn without the students thronging the place. Even the pavement dwellers had stayed away. When the place was crowded, one didn't notice how shabby the old building looked, with the graffiti and the handbills stuck on top of each other. Bondona looked at her watch.

She thought of her mother, all alone in the house, worrying about her every minute till she returned in the evening. Her face had looked hurt and sad when she retorted rudely in the morning. Poor Ma, Bondona thought, and a feeling of tenderness for her made her eyes film over . . . . She remembered how soothing, how comforting her touch was, how gentle her caress was, when she was sick, or hurt. . . .

The Psychological Level

THEY NOTICED THE TILT IN THE HOUSE ONLY AFTER THEY HAD moved in. It was Umesh Majumdar, their neighbour, who pointed it out to them. He said that he had always been aware of the tilt. In fact, the tilt was prominent only when viewed against the straightness of *his* house. One had to have a contrast to observe such things. Ever since, Madan Haldar hated Umesh Majumdar for pointing it out to him, for *contrasting* the two houses, for the *way* he said, 'I hope you are aware that your house is tilted.' As if he was laughing within himself, making fun of the house, of the fact that Madan Haldar *hadn't* known which insinuated that he had been made a fool by the previous owner. And, as if that wasn't enough, Madan Haldar also learnt that both the houses were owned by the same person, which meant that he had sold the straight one to Umesh Majumdar and the tilted one to Madan Haldar so that the former could gloat on his better luck.

Madan Haldar made enquiries. This was his only property. He had spent all his life savings on this roof over his head. O course he couldn't have done it by himself. A refugee from the partition of Bengal, or a politically displaced person, as he preferred to call himself euphemistically, he was just a retired state government employee, respectable but poor. Like a typical middle-class Bengali, he had dutifully fulfilled the role of the eldest son by taking on the burden of supporting the family and marrying off his sisters. He had never had the kind of savings needed to build a house. Yet he was proud and defiant. He would probably never have accepted his mother-in-law's offer to give him the money to buy the house, had she not, tactfully mentioned that it was to be a loan, to be repaid. So now, this tilt in the house bothered him.

In the months to come, he consulted architects and contractors, who positioned themselves at all sorts of vantage points around the house, to observe and assess this anomaly. In the end, they all agreed that although it was unusual, it wasn't dangerous. It was probably the constant vibrations caused by the passing trains that had made the foundation to settle in a certain way. The walls were checked. No cracks. No danger. Madan Haldar and his wife Shefali Haldar breathed a sigh of relief. His wife was more concerned because it was her mother's investment.

Madan Haldar now decided to give his tilted house a distinguished appearance, so that it would *contrast* with Umesh Majumdar's house. He hired the best *mistries* and bought the latest brand of paint. The colour he chose hadn't been dared by such middle-class localities yet. While most houses wore dowdy greys, or dirty whites, or dull creams, house 20/1/2 suddenly stood out like a beauty queen, in gleaming pink. It assaulted one's senses the moment it came into one's sight, like sudden pain in your teeth, when you bit into a *peda*.

What Madan Haldar hadn't calculated was that all the fuss had actually brought on more attention to the tilt. The house became kind of branded. Friends and relatives, visiting them from other parts of the city, had no problems locating the house, though it was situated within a complicated tangle of intensely narrow streets. Anyone who enquired about the Haldar house was guided faultlessly to the pink house with the tilt.

Meanwhile, Madan Haldar, relieved and free to enjoy his ownership at last, devoted himself to details, sometimes quite obsessively, to the annoyance of his wife. Shefali complained that she never had a moment's peace because some *mistri* or the other was always hanging about the house, tapping, banging, scraping, plastering, screwing, creating noise, mess and encroaching on her privacy. Madan Haldar wanted to show off to the world that his house now looked better than Umesh Majumdar's, despite the tilt.

By July, the house had more or less nothing to fix. It had come to an optimum point of perfection, except for the tilt. But that year, after ten years of relative drought, the monsoons came with a vengeance. On the 22nd, after a few days of intense heat, the midday skies suddenly rumbled and turned slate grey. By late afternoon, the heavens opened up to let down a steady downpour. Over lunch Madan Haldar grumbled that his expensive paint was being washed away.

'You should have waited till autumn,' Shefali Haldar said.

'And allowed that son-of-a-pig's house to look better?'

'It wasn't his fault, you know, that our house was built that way,' Shefali tried to reason.

That irritated Madan Haldar. How could his wife take the son-of-a-pig's side? He scowled through lunch and then went to the bedroom balcony on the first floor, to keep an eye on the rain. He was shocked to see that the rainwater, instead of going down the drain, was rolling back towards the bedroom and flowing over the low cement barrier. It was obviously that the tilt of the house was causing this to happen. Saris, towels, pyjamas and sheets were stuffed behind the barrier to keep the room from flooding.

By late afternoon, it was apparent that the entire area was experiencing a flood and the rains still showed no signs of letting. Madan Haldar spent his time rushing from window to balcony and then from the ground floor porch to the terrace on the second floor. First, the deeper sides of the lane filled up, leaving people to walk in the middle, trying their best not to get their feet and clothes wet.

'Dada, how much water that side?' he kept asking people who were passing by. As if, more water *that side* was some kind of consolation. In the beginning, everyone said that the other side was worse. Then as the lane started filling up, causing people to walk gingerly over the spine, Madan Haldar worried how long the rains would continue.

Shefali Haldar had always loved the monsoons. Like Tagore, she thought of the season as one which made lovers pine for each other. Her favourite pastime as a young girl had been to lie close to the window and allow the spray from the rains to wet her lightly. It gave her a refreshing, tingly sensation and brought on shivers and goose bumps. But then, she had never had to worry about paints being washed away, or competing with neighbours for the best-looking-house satisfaction. As her husband rushed from terrace to porch and back, trying to keep track of the rainwater, which was actually drainwater, because the rain water couldn't get through the choked drains, she tuned into *Akashbani Kolkata*.

The song being aired was one of her favourite monsoon songs of Tagore, '*Mono Mor Megher Shongi*', which spoke of the poet's mind flying away with the rain clouds. She hummed along with Hemonto Chattopadhyay's voice. It went well with the pouring sound outside. The gentle, melodious voice, the coolness of the air and her own exhaustion, made her doze off.

She was rudely woken up by Madan Haldar who was shaking her and shouting, 'Get up! Wake up! The water is almost entering our house!' He had already switched off the radio.

The sound of the rains which had seemed so musical at first, now sounded like bombardment, and much too close for comfort. Too real and loud, like surround sound. 'Jham-jham-jham-jham,' it went, 'Jham-jham-jham-jham.' Monotonous, claustrophobic. . . .

The rain had started four hours ago. Now it was five in the evening. Shefali Haldar shivered. The atmosphere seemed saturated with moisture. Everything felt wet—the bed, her clothes, her hair. She rushed out to the balcony and looked down. The narrow lane, which would normally be occupied by the kids of the neighbourhood, playing cricket, now looked like some scene from a movie about natural disaster. Black, oily water swirled and coiled around the narrow lane like a giant serpent. It was thick and heavy, as if it had all intentions of staying exactly where it was, forever.

And still, 'Jham-jham-jham-jham. . . .'

A rickshaw appeared round the corner, carrying a man, obviously returning from office. He was sitting awkwardly, under the patched-up hood, with his shoes and socks in hand, yet fully clothed, including an immaculately knotted navy blue tie. Instead of the usual grating sound of the wheels, it made quiet splish-splash sounds, with every step of the rickshaw puller, who wore a blue plastic bag to protect his head, though his vest and lungi were soaked and stuck to his sinuous body like a second skin. The drag and pull of the rickshaw created heavy waves, which climbed up the wall of the opposite house to a certain height and rolled down, leaving wet marks.

Looking down, Shefali felt seasick. She went down to make some tea. It was like going down from the deck into the bowels of a ship. She was just about to wash the cups, when Madan Haldar appeared.

'Don't turn on the tap!' he cried out in panic.

'Why?'

Shefali looked at the tap in alarm, as if it was a wild beast.

'It will add to the water level outside,' he said.

Madan and Shefali Haldar spent the next hour in the ground floor balcony, conversing with people passing by. Everyone seemed to be used to the phenomenon. It gradually became apparent that theirs was a low-lying area, due to its close proximity to the high railway tracks and whenever the rains were heavy, there was waterlogging. All the houses in the neighbourhood had specially raised foundations, so that the water couldn't enter inside. In the front side of their house, it looked as if the water wouldn't reach the short flight of steps, though every passing car and rickshaw created black, heavy waves, that climbed the first stair and then went down, leaving it wet, like a warning. However, Madan Haldar, who had been checking every side of the house continuously, pointed out the possibility that the water may enter from the back entrance, where due to the tilt the water level was already touching the first step and wave-warning the second one.

There was nothing left for them to do but to pray for the rains to stop. As darkness descended, with the dank smell of the stagnant drainwater rising from the streets and permeating the house, Madan Haldar prayed that the water inundated Umesh Majumdar's house. But the heavens seemed to have some other deep, vindictive plan. The darkness outside, the black encircling waters and the colourless downpour, became one giant communion 'Jham-jham-jham-jham'. The Akashbani forecast was that it would rain throughout the night.

At exactly ten past seven, the water level crossed Madan Haldar's *psychological barrier*. It swallowed the second step at the back entrance. By that time they even stopped using the bathroom, lest they add to the water level. From their sinking ship they watched helplessly, as exactly around 7.30 p.m., it entered the house, from underneath the locked backdoor. It filled up the landing, and then inched towards the corridor. Due to the tilt, the ceiling now appeared slanted, including the seaside painting from Digha.

Soon the water heaved upwards, the splish-splash of small waves making curved wet marks on Madan Haldar's freshly painted walls and entering their tastefully decorated drawing room. There, in a weird swirl, it lifted up the lighter cane chairs and fondly moved them around, like babies wanting to be carried. The splish-splash now caught within a closed area, echoed up the staircase, to the bedroom. Madan Haldar listened to the sounds lying on his bed and staring up at the ceiling with unblinking eyes.

Around 8 p.m., there was a loud banging on the back door and Umesh Majumdar's loud booming voice penetrated the 'jham-jham', breaking the silence of the room.

'Madan Babu! Madan Babu! It seems the water has entered your house. Do you need any help? Some food, maybe. . . .'

Upstairs, a bedroom window was thrust open and a hard, rubber Bata sandal went hissing through the air like a boomerang towards a figure standing knee-deep in water, with the lungi folded upwards and tucked at the waist.

Living to Eat

I NEVER UNDERSTOOD THIS BANGAAL OBSESSION ABOUT FOOD. Whenever they met, they would go on and on about what they used to eat back there in East Bengal. It seems that nothing, absolutely nothing could compare with the quality or the size or the plentitude of fruit, vegetable, fish or confectionery that they had been used to, especially the fish. Ah, they all missed their *Padma'r Ilish* badly. Not that this silvery fish wasn't available in Calcutta. Come monsoon, it would become our staple at least for a month. Fried or steamed with mustard paste, cooked lightly or chutney made with its eggs, or a vegetable dish perked up with hilsa heads. Every bit of the hilsa fish was tasty. But I refuse to admit that these hilsas from the Ganges were any less tasty than the ones from the Padma. At least to me it was so. But one never dared to even suggest such a thing to those people who had grown up in the land of the mighty rivers.

Amulyada, our servant from Midnapore, had a tough job. He would have to go to the market everyday, with his two cloth-bags rolled up, one for fish, the other one for vegetable, the money clenched in his fist and a mind that was already getting prepared for the deluge of dissatisfaction he would have to face for what he had bought with the money. Things had already started to become difficult for the average man in those days. His fixed salary couldn't match up to the soaring inflation. And the daily shopping was becoming lighter and lighter. He would return with a grim face, dump the fish in the non-vegetarian kitchen, the vegetables in grandma's kitchenette and flop down on the floor with a sigh. '*Kaliyug* has arrived,' he would declare with a voice of doom, as grandma rummaged through the vegetable with an expression of disgust. His favourite baseline was, 'What do you expect, when the end of life on earth has already begun?' It was actually his defence mechanism to divert the blame onto some vague unknown factor. Though Amulyada had the habit of stealing a few rupees from the grocery money to pay for his bidis, he was never taken to task for it.

'Amulya, it is still two rupees short!' my mother would mildly insist, as she tried to tally the items and their prices in her *hisheb* notebook. But it was impossible to pin him down, as he was adept at altering per seer prices and the weight measure.

Then would follow the tiresome routine in which grandma would examine and reject everything, saying there was nothing in it for her to cook. She insisted that if there was raw jackfruit or raw papaya or banana flower, there had to be coconut along with it, or else there was no way she could cook it. She never adjusted to the fact that coconuts were expensive in Calcutta.

It wasn't like in Dhaka, where they had coconut trees in their own garden. 'Where is my garam masala? How can I cook without garam masala?' or, 'Where is the *vadi* to go with the *lau*?' She was, of course, a great cook and like all great cooks, she was fussy about her ingredients. She needed raisins for her chutney and cashew nuts for her sweet preparations. And the grumbling would just go on and on till everyone had eaten and would say over and over again, how good everything had tasted because of her magical touch. She was indeed a sorceress when it came to the art of cooking and even without most of her ingredients, she could make everything taste heavenly. But the constant wistful references to her golden days never stopped. She never allowed herself to settle down into reduced circumstances, never gracefully adjusted to her new life. She had an elephant's memory and could recall to the minutest detail, her life before Calcutta. She hadn't forgotten a single name, a single incident or a single date. But the trigger that turned on her memories was food. I shall forever wonder what a real *bakarkhani* or a *balushai* would taste like. Nor would I know the difference between a *dhakai amriti* or *langcha* and our humble Calcutta versions. And what exactly, was a *dhakai parota*? But when those people met, their ecstatic recall of memories would rematerialise those things, making them seem food of the gods.

It is sad that I could never share their sense of loss. How could I know what it felt like to be forced out of one's own country, one's home and land? I was born and brought up in my own motherland India, independent, well protected by a stable and modern state, a fairly well-established family. How could I feel the pain of losing one's property, job, school, college, childhood friends and the familiar surroundings in which one had grown up, like a plant that had matured from a seed to a large tree, in the same familiar piece of earth, and then suddenly uprooted? They mourned, remembering the lush green fields where they ran barefoot; the ponds and busy waterways where boats and steamers had plied and where they had fished and swam; the fresh air and the robust lifestyle; the *bhatiyali* songs reverberating over the vast expanses of waters as the *majhis* cruised on their boats; the noisy and raucous East Bengali dialects; the raw, earthy jokes of the tangawallas and fish sellers; the ominous beauty of the monsoons that burst the riverbanks and flooded vast areas; and above all, the fiery cuisine. I think, what hurt most about their displacement, was their total loss of status. Rich or poor, they had had a place in their own society. In West Bengal, they were just 'refugees'—a stigma that was all the more difficult to live down, because they had had no desire to come, anyway. 'Those dirty refugees, who came in hordes and made a mess of our city' were undercurrents that persisted and sometimes surfaced in polite society. Proud, that my father's family was, they never allowed anyone to live down such remarks. They had their own ways of ridiculing the *ghotis*, the name they had given the locals of West Bengal, for what reason, I do not know. They ridiculed their lack of physical stamina, the blandness of their cuisine, their lack of enterprise and their docile existence.

There's a story my father often enjoyed telling, about how he had once dropped by at a friend's house after a football match. They were ghotis and his friend's mother served those special miniature *luchis* that local people made, along with a small helping of potato curry. The size of the luchis was so small, compared to the ones the Bangaals made, that my father referred to them as dolls' luchis. He was so hungry that he put all six of them on top of each other and as his friend's mother looked on, shocked, he put the whole bunch into his mouth and devoured it at one go.

'What could I do?' he would mock, 'Here I was, ravenously hungry after football practice and she expected me to daintily nibble at her dolls' luchis one by one?'

Naturally, the lady had to enquire politely whether he needed any more, to which my father nodded vigorously, thus sending the poor lady off into a sweaty double session of kneading, rolling-out and frying.

'She must have dreaded the prospect of my dropping by at their house,' my father chuckled wickedly.

The habits of an active and robust lifestyle died hard on these vigorous people. They all spoke of eating big, though I never got to witness any gastronomical feats. I remember my grandfather as a big man, but he lived only a few years after my birth. So I had no way of verifying his professed capacity to eat *an entire goat*! But such verbal extravagances were also a part of the Bangaal ethos.

One of our ghoti relatives, by virtue of having married into our family, aptly described this East Bengali obsession with food. Not being too particular about what he ate, as long as his hunger was satisfied, he committed the ultimate sacrilege of pouring in different items at random from the bowls that had been carefully placed one after the other, in the exact sequence in which they were supposed to be eaten, and then mixing them up on his plate. My father, who was the perfect gourmet, a connoisseur of fine food, who ate like he was performing some elaborate ritual, flinched at this barbaric act.

'Ish!' he exclaimed, 'You have spoiled everything! *Shukto* must be eaten before daal. Now, how will you get the delicate taste of the Lau? . . . and the aroma of the fish head in the daal will be spoilt by the bitter taste of. . . .'

He listened, totally bewildered at this poetry and science of food. Then said, 'You know, Dada, the trouble with you people is that you live to eat. I eat, to live.'

But the man had already and utterly fallen in the family's esteem, for being such an insensitive eater.

There was a time, when the situation in Bengal suddenly deteriorated drastically. Everything was strictly rationed and black-marketing thrived. Even Haringhata milk became scarce. There were queues everywhere—ration shops, kerosene outlets, coal shops, milk booths. I remember a Bengali song of those days. It went something like,

'Everywhere you go, there are lines,
And then there are fines
For breaking those lines...'

It was a time when Bengalis had to change their food habits drastically, like having chapattis instead of rice for dinner; *Dalia*, or split wheat became a part of many family diets and one began to hear about strange new preparations, like '*Kanchkolar Chop*'. These were the days when my grandmother almost stopped eating because she couldn't swallow the poor quality parboiled rice that was supplied through the ration shops. The whole family developed a new pastime, sitting with thalis of rice or daal, picking out miniscule stone chips and other rubbish with which they had been adulterated. Even then, occasionally, we would inadvertently bite into a chip or two, which had been too colourless to have been noticed. Many of us damaged our teeth during those days. All these changes doubly encouraged my elderly relatives to dream about their golden past.

A large part of my aunt's remembrances of Dhaka, concerned the exploits of her brothers, especially my father. Their summer afternoon forays into neighbouring gardens, up mango trees, gorging on those juicy fruits; their monsoon fishing adventures, when rivers and ponds overflowed, bringing out the fish into the flooded fields; their novel ways of stealing *pithes* from grandma's kitchen; and the ingenious device of the *paat* straw which was pushed down into the milk *saraas*, so the layer of cream on top would not break, while they sucked up the rich milk.

Some of these stories seemed unbelievable when attributed to my uncles, who seemed models of perfect behaviour and very serious to me.

The most popular of all my uncles who lived in Delhi and visited once a year during school holidays, had the passion for food mixed with an amazing generosity of heart. He was fun from the word go. For a month every year, our house became an endless picnic spot, a food festival centre, a free hotel, where friends and relatives, even the most vaguely and remotely connected, would turn up, having got wind of his arrival. Every morning he would go off to the market, where each shopkeeper greeted him like an old friend and he would return with what the neighbours thought must be the whole market, on the head of a hired coolie, and a very proud Amulyada in tow. It never occurred to my uncle that bringing home all that stuff put an enormous strain on the ladies of the house, who had to sort, peel, chop, throughout the day, as the cook laboured to prepare everything before lunchtime. But no one complained. They knew it was his innate generosity of spirit that made him want to buy the best fish, meat and vegetable in the market, regardless of the cost. He ate very little himself but made it a point to supervise the cooking and be around when the ladies and children ate, selecting his favourite pieces for each one, or forcing an extra helping on someone. It just gave him immense satisfaction to watch people eat well.

'Now, let me show you,' he would offer, when I, or my cousin found it difficult to pick the fine bones from the fish, or suck out the marrow from the bones of mutton.

There was no way one could avoid overeating with my uncle around. One would be forced to do it just to please him. We just loved the atmosphere he created around us once a year—a climate of plenty, a season of bounty. Amulyada for once, would be in heaven, basking in the aura of prosperity, as he followed my uncle from shop to shop, free from the trauma of having to scrimp and trying to make the limited money stretch and from the awareness that he would have to account for every penny he spent. During those few days, he would walk tall in the market, feeling like a royal assistant, sniffing scornfully at the same shopkeepers who insulted him everyday, when he haggled with them. To him, my uncle was the nearest thing to God.

Those days are gone now. Most of those real East Bengalis have passed away. On the day of my grandmother's *shraadh*, my uncle returned from the market, crying like a baby. It seems, he had felt her footsteps following him to each stall, guiding him, and sometimes, goading him to buy things she liked to eat.

Banshi

THERE IS NO SINGLE WORD THAT CAN DESCRIBE BANSHI, NOR, a thousand. The Sanyal family will never forget this curious man who was an integral part of their lives for over ten years. And those who never met him have missed an interesting experience.

Mr Sanyal called him the 'missing link'. Probably because of the way he looked—like an ape who had progressed too far into the process of homo-sapienisation to regress to his original state. He was short, stocky and hairy; his arms hung from his shoulders so far down that he could easily scratch his feet without bending, if he wanted to. He gave the impression that he might just grab a window grill and start swinging from it. And once, that is exactly what happened, or so Mahua, the Sanyals' twelve-year-old daughter would have us believe.

'Ma, please don't send Banshida to my school anymore. I'll come on my own,' Mahua begged, as soon as the old servant had put down her school satchel on her study table and gone out of the room.

Her mother stopped her knitting and raised her eyebrows.

'The schoolbag is heavy. How will you carry it on your own?'

'I'll do it, Ma. I'll do it. *PLEASE*?' she implored, flinging herself petulantly on her mother and making a mess of her knitting.

'Now look what you've done,' she said crossly.

Then she rolled up her knitting and put it aside, curious to learn what Banshi had done this time. Mahua did bring in stories of Banshi's funny deeds from time to time and they usually had some good laughs at Banshi's expense. For instance, the way he had tied up his sandals to his feet with a coconut fibre rope because they kept slipping out. Or the way he sometimes carried her heavy satchel on his head like a street hawker, drawing stares from people.

'Ma, he climbed up the front gate of the school and started hollering out my name, while we were waiting inside!' she said with disgust.

Her mother suppressed a smile.

'Then what happened?' she asked, trying to visualise the scene in front of the stylish school building, where most girls had uniformed chauffeurs waiting for them to come out. She desperately tried to keep a straight face for Mahua's sake.

'Everyone started laughing and pointing out to him . . . I felt so embarrassed,' Mahua said tearfully.

'Well, did you answer?'

She looked guiltily at her mother.

'I felt so ashamed that I pretended I didn't know him. Thank God he called me *guria*, or my friends would have come to know he was my servant.'

'Then? Didn't he spot you?'

'No,' Mahua said with a sly gleam in her eyes, 'I quietly went and hid in the toilet till everyone had gone. When I came out I found him crouching outside the gate . . . like a monkey!' she said, trying to find the right word to describe him.

'Now, now, Mahua, don't say things like that about Banshida,' Mrs Sanyal scolded. 'He loves you and cares so much about you.'

Banshi was an embarrassment alright, but life in the Sanyal household would not be the same without him. Whatever derogatory term Mr Sanyal might have used to describe him, his wife Namita never forgot for a single day her debt to him.

As an officer in West Bengal government's Food Department, Mr Sanyal had been posted to a remote district near the Bengal-Bihar border. He had to go without his family because of Mahua's school. So it was Banshi who accompanied him, to cook and housekeep. That was a wise decision, as it turned out later. Had he not been there, Mr Sanyal would not have survived. In the harsh conditions of the undeveloped district, he went down with a severe case of gastroenteritis, a disease that wiped out hundreds of people that monsoon. Banshi nursed him with such devotion that he became quite a legend among the family of officers. Many years later, Namita tried returning the favour by nursing Banshi during his last days.

When Mahua and her mother came down for a month's visit during summer vacation, they were wonderstruck by his knowledge of the countryside and its flora and fauna. He knew how to keep the deadly *shankhachud* snakes out of the house by sprinkling bleaching powder around the house. When the gardener was bit by a scorpion, Banshi hurriedly pulled out a spiky plant from the garden and applied its crushed leaves on the wound. It instantly relieved the man's burning pain. In a place full of strange creatures like centipedes and geckos and chameleons and scary 'aeroplane insects', which sounded like droning aircrafts and had teeth as sharp as saw-edges; the spidery matter that burst out of cottonseeds and glided around, making Mahua scream in terror and run for her life; and monkeys that marauded their kitchen when no one was looking, Banshi seemed to fit into the scene like another strange species in a wild landscape.

In fact, he had his own unique ways of dealing with every problem. He never killed or threatened anything. If a monkey bothered Mahua, he would go down on his knees and clasping his hands respectfully, pray to Lord Rama's friends to leave. And indeed, the monkeys would troop out as if they understood. If anything, it reinforced Mr Sanyal's observation on the unique position of Banshi in the progress of the human species.

Banshi's hairiness came in for a lot of flak. It was the bane of his existence, sprouting from every orifice in his body—his ears, his nostrils and every conceivable part of him. So whenever they found a grayish-white strand lying around anywhere, they knew exactly where it had come from because he was the only graying human around. But Banshi had his own insouciant way of dealing with their accusations. Once, Mr Sanyal held up a suspicious-looking specimen from the gravy and asked Banshi to identify what it was. Far from being embarrassed, he peered at it with his weak eyes and then with a scornful sniff of his nose, gave his unabashed verdict.

'Oh, that! It's just a piece of thread!'

The very next day, Mr Sanyal appointed a barber to come every fortnight and give Banshi a clean shave, which under his specifications included his ears, nose, armpits as well as his chest.

The strangest thing about Banshi was his age. He seemed to be suspended in a time-warp, never growing older. It was no use asking him how old he was. The truth was that he had absolutely no idea. Nor did he have any concept of numbers or counting. When Mr Sanyal was posted back to Calcutta, he begged him to give him a peon's job in the Food Department. But when he had to fill up his age, he said well, it was something like thirty, thirty-five or even forty! No one probed the impossibility, though he clearly looked more than fifty, giving him the benefit of working a little longer. So, Banshi never retired. He died before he reached the mandatory age.

Banshi was so much fun that no one in the Sanyal household ever questioned the improbabilities of his life. His *desh* was in Orissa and every three to four years he would pack up his tin suitcase to much beyond its capacity, with all the big-town goodies he could lay his hands on; then, borrowing more money he could possibly repay in five years, head for home. They smirked about his relationship with his wife, who they felt, must hold Banshi in total remote control from the deepest little village in Orissa. He seemed to live for his wife and daughter. From the descriptions he provided, the woman seemed young and beautiful and had desires that left poor Banshi breathless to fulfil. To his credit, and to the amusement of his family, he never let her down. He was indeed an exemplary specimen of a hen-pecked husband. From all the precious gifts he took for her, they gathered that she must have pretty expensive tastes for a village belle. Jewellery, saris, confectioneries, perfumes, tonics—you name it, Banshi took it for her. But the most extraordinary thing about his family was his daughter. She was the apple of his eyes, his very heartbeat. Only thing was, she had been born on a year preceded by two years during which Banshi hadn't visited his desh. He was so overjoyed by the news of her birth, that no one had the heart to point out to him that there had to be something amiss.

The most hilarious thing about Banshi though, was his accent. It was a cross between Oriya, his mother tongue and an East Bengali dialect which he picked up during his youth spent in Chittagong. Nobody knew how he landed up there, but as a young lad he had worked in Mr Sanyal's ancestral home when his parents were alive. Like many people during the Partition, he had disappeared, and then resurfaced in Calcutta, where his quest for a job brought him back to the Sanyal household. This time of course, Mr Sanyal's parents were dead and it took a while for the son to recognise a much older Banshi.

Banshi's return to the household was therefore looked upon as a matter of destiny and he was treated with a certain respect, a kind of indulgence that the other part-time servants could not command. These younger menials resented this 'attitude', and questioned the authority with which he ordered them around. The Sanyals had rewarded him for his past services by building him a small outhouse and he loved ruling over his domain. He ordered the maid to clean his room, the sweeper to clean his toilet and the cook to put more chillies in his curries.

It was therefore with deep mourning that the Sanyals bade their final goodbye to this trusted and loyal servant ten years later. It happened after his sudden decision to visit his desh on a second successive year—something he could never afford to do financially. Surprised, that he would spend so much money again, the family tried to dissuade him. Especially, since it was in the middle of one of the worst monsoons that had hit the Orissa coastline. The journey, they warned, would be hazardous, to say the least, with washed-away roads and no proper transport plying. But Banshi was adamant. It had something to do with the letter he had received but he never divulged the real reason. His office threatened to sack him as he had no accumulated leave and still being a temporary staff. His moneylender threatened he wouldn't give him any until he had repaid his previous debts. But nothing could stop Banshi from going. He was as stubborn as a mule.

When Banshi returned after a month, he looked ghastly and sick. Alarmed, they called in the doctor. But it was already too late. Banshi died soon, without explanations, without repaying his debts, without the slightest fight. It was as if he had lost his will to live and that he had returned just to die.

Crowds of stunned mourners thronged their house; people from his office, from the neighbourhood; people he knew in the nearby market. Indeed, the poor illiterate Oriya servant was a legend at death. Mrs Sanyal who had kept a constant vigil at his bedside, was inconsolable. It was as if she had lost a close relative.

The real story of Banshi, however, came out many months later, when a young bumpkin knocked on their door and in halting Bengali mixed with strong Oriya accents, demanded to see his *baap*.

He had indeed come prepared, with a small bundle of clothes, to stay in his father's house and was surprised that it was only a small room, outside the main building. More than the news of his father's death, it was the size of his modest quarters that came as a rude shock to him and he looked around with suspicion at the rest of the house and its inhabitants, as if they were intruders who had taken over what rightfully belonged to him. It was clear that the country bumpkin had very misinformed ideas about his father's occupation in Calcutta. What became evident after much questioning was that he had come to enquire why the monthly money orders had stopped.

Surprised at discovering that Banshi had a grown-up son he had chosen never to mention, Mrs Sanyal thought it was time to do some digging. The story that unfolded was so weird that she wished she hadn't wanted to know.

The young man expressed his outrage the moment the topic of Banshi's daughter was brought up. It was obviously a very sensitive issue, because the wife and daughter that Banshi had talked about and lived for, were neither real nor legitimate. It was unbelievable, but it seems Banshi had led a double life all along. His real wife, the bumpkin's mother, still lived in their ancestral village, tending the small rice field and few cows they owned. Now old and weak, she heavily depended on her son and the monthly money orders that Banshi used to send.

According to him, the 'other woman', whom he called a prostitute and a witch, amongst other names, had seduced his father and had been trying to pass on the daughter she had had by another man, as his own. Belonging to the Devadasi clan of the past, she was beautiful and held his father in thrall. Mesmerised by her, he had long ago stopped living with his real family, though he continued providing for them.

Why had Banshi returned to his desh in a hurry? What was the letter he had received just before leaving? Well, the bumpkin provided an answer to that as well, and without the slightest regret. He said he had written the letter himself, emphasising that he had decided to take revenge on the siren woman and provide justice for his ageing mother. He had written to tell his father the truth, he justified himself, because the woman was trying to deprive his real family of their rightful share. He said he had been forced to take action because of the rumours she was spreading, saying that Banshi had promised to marry her soon.

'All she wanted was his money!' he said angrily, 'So she lied to him, saying the daughter was his. I had to do something,' he said, 'to protect my mother.'

'Poor Banshi!' Mrs Sanyal sighed, relating the story to her husband later.

'He must have been devastated.'

'You always had a soft spot for Banshi, didn't you?' Mr Sanyal teased his wife, 'Would you have forgiven anybody else for leaving his wife for a younger woman?'

'Absolutely not,' she replied pointedly.

'But Banshi was not anybody else. He was special.'

Cousin Indrajit

Rita went to Roydon High, the most exclusive girls' school in the city, which prided itself in providing a protective and orthodox environment to its students. Though their boys' section was situated on the corner of the same road, the two sections might as well have been separate institutions, they were so deliberately segregated. Even their socials and fétes were held separately. However, deprived of the company of the boys, the girls learnt to make up for it by fantasising about them. Some of the girls even mastered the art of eye-contact, through the windows facing the street.

At lunchtime, they eagerly crowded the windows, chattering and restless like birds in cages, their eyes seeking out the Roydon boys standing in clusters under the gulmohur tree, on the other side of the street. Sometimes, the impossible did happen and against all odds, just two pairs of eyes would succeed in mating, through the impersonal distance of the busy street. But lunchtime was an ephemeral space-time for any conclusive event to take place and the sound of the bell would oll like a cruel death knell for desperate lovers through space. The eyes would be forced to tear apart and many a longing carried away in the painfully fluttering hearts, to afternoon periods of sheer misery.

Of course, the eye-romances never got very far. The simple reason being, the owners of those passionate eyes never, ever had any chance to meet in person. The iron gates of Roydon Girls' were higher and more formidable than the Bastille. The six school buses left from inside the compound and returned back, inside. Their reputation as a strict, upper class girls' school, kept them out of reach of most of the city boys.

Though the parents of these children preferred to bring up their kids in this way, which they considered 'respectable', Rita's mother had begun to think that maybe, Rita was too under-exposed. Not having a brother or even a male cousin to grow up around, she was almost painfully shy and appeared uncomfortable and even awkward, when introduced to sons of friends and acquaintances. It just wasn't healthy, she worried.

Lolita, on the other hand, came from the opposite side of he social spectrum, though she lived in the same Alipore neighbourhood. She was definitely not the kind of girl these parents would have liked their children to be friends with. Lolita's parents, who had met and married during their days with the NA, led a liberated lifestyle that made it difficult for them to be accepted by mainly the upper-middle-class Bengalis. Hushed gossip was common among the ladies of the neighbourhood about the noisy parties they held, the kind of people they mixed with, the kind of clothes they wore and even their diet. But one couldn't blame these moms for being critical of their daughter Lolita. At sixteen, she wore imported, coloured bras that made their presence obvious under the thin cotton dresses. Rita often wondered whether her lips were naturally red or she used lipstick. Lipstick! Even her mother used it rarely. She just had one muted shade that she gingerly applied and then promptly wiped off with the end of her sari, so it wouldn't look obvious, that too only on those rare occasions when she went out with her father to office parties, wearing chiffon saris with a strand of pearls dangling around her neck.

Lolita's problem with boys was that she had too many in her life. She had at least a dozen boyfriends, who picked her up on their noisy bikes and her psyche was loaded with Mills and Boon romances. According to most women of Alipore, Lolita was beyond redemption, just like the Anglo-Indian girls who went to Bishop Prescott School with her. But Rita's mother was beginning to wonder whether her own daughter was the other extreme.

The letter had arrived out of the blue. Rita's father had just one sister and they hadn't heard from her for years. Of course, they talked about her during the last war with Pakistan, as her husband was in the army. But a letter from her sister-in-law during peace time was a bit of a surprise for Rita's mother.

'Bimala di's coming!' she declared with excitement to the neighbourhood ladies, who had gathered for an afternoon chat at their house.

They came regularly because Rita's mother made excellent coconut *naroos* and also because from the porch of this house, they had the best possible view of the flat where Lolita and her parents lived. The view, though, was restricted to their heavily-draped drawing room, where according to them all the action was. Rita's mother hadn't really seen any extraordinary action but then, even ladies were entitled to their own fantasies.

Rita knew that a letter had come from her *pishimoni*, from Srinagar, where her uncle was stationed. Now, as she passed the ladies on her way, she heard something that made her linger behind the curtains.

'Her son has completed school and will go to college, here.'

'Is that so!' one of the ladies exclaimed. 'Bimaladi's son would now be going to college—how time flies! Last time they came, she was taking him to Darjeeling, remember, to admit him to St. Paul's. He was just a little boy then.'

'Oh, I believe he's now a very handsome young man!' Rita's mother said.

Rita tried to remember pishimoni's son. She must have been only five, then, when they were in Calcutta the last time.

All she could remember was that he was a thin, restless boy, with almost all his front teeth missing.

She couldn't understand why her heart beat so wildly at the thought of her handsome cousin, or why she was eavesdropping, for that matter. She quickly fled, as the ladies changed the topic.

Pishimoni was the most pleasant sight Rita had ever seen. With her rich, protein complexion, her mass of black, permed hair, bright lipstick and green and yellow printed Japanese georgette draped carelessly, she was a vision of charm and beauty, right out of the tambola-playing, permissive military club. Rita noticed how drab and unfashionable her mother looked beside her.

'Oh, my!' pishimoni said, with the broadest of smiles, 'Is this our Ritu? What a lady she has become!'

Then, she turned around and addressed the strapping six-feet-something young man, who had been standing quietly behind her.

'Indra beta, you remember Ritu? This is your cousin, Ritu. How fast they grow!' she said again, in amazement.

At seventeen, Indrajit was a spitting image of his athletic father. His cheeks still held the ruddy glow of the Darjeeling cold. The smart St. Paul blazer with its shiny brass buttons outlined the muscles that had been bred by gym training and cross-country running.

'Hello, Rita,' cousin Indrajit said, slightly bending his form and offering his hand. Maybe it was the anglicised way he pronounced her name, with the emphasis on the first syllable that made Rita start and look up at him. His eyes, dark, shining and mysterious, immediately locked onto hers.

Rita's mouth went dry.

'Hullo,' she managed feebly, avoiding his full gaze. Then, mumbling something, she ran into her room, without taking his hand.

'She's a little shy,' her mother apologised.

'Why did you run away?'

Rita jumped and turned.

The terrace was dark, under a totally moonless December sky but she recognised the silhouette of cousin Indrajit. He stood with his hands in his pockets, leaning against the door. Again, she felt her heart going wild. Could he have known she was up here and followed her?

'Run away?' she asked, pretending she didn't know what he was talking about.

Indrajit took his hands out of his pockets and walked up to the ledge where she was standing.

'I have a feeling you're avoiding me,' he said, watching her, sideways.

A breeze shook the leaves, making a dry, rustling noise and emphasising the silence of the night. Rita wished she had something to cover herself with. Her mother would have been aghast to see her standing here uncovered, on a December night. Though it was quite dark, she could feel his eyes peering into hers.

'Why should I avoid you?'

She looked up at the black sky, desperately searching for a star to focus on.

'You're prettier than I had imagined,' he said.

'I have to go.'

Rita started walking towards the door.

'No, don't go yet.'

He stretched a strong arm and caught her hand.

'Someone will hear us and we'll be in trouble,' Rita whispered.

'Everyone's gone to bed. I checked.'

For a few seconds, neither of them spoke. Suddenly Rita shivered.

'Cold?' he asked, putting his arm around her shoulders. Rita shrank a little from the touch but didn't move away. There was a heady feeling about this and the more wrong all this felt, more she wanted to be drawn into it.

'Did you know I was up here?' she asked, still looking away from him.

'No. But I searched you out.'

'Why?'

'Because,' he replied, turning her face towards him and looking into her eyes, 'I knew you wanted me to.'

Then, without any warning, he bent down and kissed her on the lips. Rita drew in her breath sharply, in surprise.

'I can tell, it was your first kiss,' Indrajit smiled, still holding her.

'How?'

'I just know,' he said, quizzically.

'Do you go around kissing girls?'

'You are so innocent,' he laughed. Then, sensing her discomfort, 'Oh, no, nothing to worry about. It's quite refreshing to me, actually.'

'Then you have kissed many girls.'

Rita wriggled out of his arms and stood apart. Her voice had sounded reproachful and cousin Indrajit hadn't missed it.

'What's wrong?'

'We have to go,' she said.

'Why?'

'Because it's morning, and we should be sleeping now.'

'Who told you that it's morning?' Indrajit said, following her to the door.

'The crows,' she replied, drawing his attention to a distant commotion, which sounded like the advance of an army. 'When they're awake, it's morning,' she said.

'I think, it's got nothing to do with the crows. I think you're angry.'

Rita led the way silently.

'I hope you didn't take this seriously,' he pursued, 'After all, we're cousins.'

They had tiptoed down the staircase in darkness but jus as they reached the landing, the light came on and Rita's mother stood at her bedroom door, squinting in surprise a the culprits.

'Cousin Indra wanted to see the terrace,' Rita blurted ou the first thing that came to her mind.

'It's nice,' Indrajit added foolishly.

'At this hour of the night? I thought you were both i your beds!'

'We were. But we couldn't sleep, so we thought . . . ' Rita' voice trailed off, unable to think too far.

'Off to bed! Off to bed! Both of you!' her mother cu her short, not wanting to draw the attention of the entir household.

As they dashed towards their respective bedrooms, the lady paused for thought. Had she caught a glimpse of something there? Couldn't be. . . They were after all cousins. Even then strange things have happened among cousins and one couldn' be too careful, she worried. Oh, what a typical mother I am she scolded herself, trying to go back to sleep. Yesterday was worried that Rita was so shy. Now that she's got over he shyness, I worry about that, too.

POSTSCRIPT

Meanwhile at Roydon Girls', the lunchtime eye-romances came to an abrupt end, when none other than Mother Superio caught one of the girls red-handed. Henceforth, the lunch-breaks became lunch-*periods*, with one or the other Sisters supervising the windows, while the girls sat at their desks, facing the blackboard and munching their sandwiches.

Rita and cousin Indrajit didn't have any more nocturnal trysts. Then, one day, she caught a glimpse of him kissing Lolita in their heavily-draped drawing room. The curtains seemed to have been pulled back deliberately, or so it seemed to Rita.

That night, she made the following entry in her diary, part of which got washed out even as she wrote. It read: 'I have learnt never to trust men, ever. I hate men and shall never, ever, fall in love or get married.'

Indrajit left as abruptly as he had arrived. His parents decided it would be better for him to join the Military Academy in Dehradun. He just didn't seem to be cut out for civilian life. Amen, said the ladies of the neighbourhood, who were getting alarmed at his prolonged presence.

But despite the entry in the diary, for almost a year after her first kiss, Rita daydreamed as she munched sandwiches under the watchful eyes of Sister, wondering if cousin Indrajit would have kissed her again, had Lolita not been around with her lipstick and coloured bras.

The Shadow

Things had been changing fast in Indira's life, ever since her fourteenth birthday. Suddenly, everyone in the family was serious about her, lots of whispering between Ma and *Thakuma* and instructions at every step.

'Now you are a big girl, Indu. Don't sit like that.'

'Cover your legs, Indu, when you're lying down. It doesn't look nice.'

'Now, don't run up and down. It doesn't look dignified.'

Most of her favourite, comfortable clothes were packed away because they were deemed unsuitable for her new time of life. No sleeveless, no tight dresses, no short skirts. She felt lumpy, uncomfortable and unclean.

Often, she would run up to *Bapi*, like she had done since she was a baby, but his usual reflexes too, seemed to have gone dead. He was like a stranger who had forgotten his cues. She would linger for a few moments, as if to encourage him to continue where he had left off. But he never scooped her up onto his lap and never kissed her the way he used to. Instead, he avoided looking at her and would say something formal that would make it impossible for things to resume the old way.

Everything that she did nowadays, made her feel like a criminal. She wasn't sure if it was okay to walk into Thakuma's puja room, anytime she wanted to, like before and help her make garlands or sandalwood paste. Once when she was there, Ma had shot in through the door and pushed her out before she even knew what had happened.

'Don't touch anything!' she had admonished. 'For five days, when you get your periods, don't enter this room. Understand?'

No, she had not understood. Indira had shut herself in her room and cried a lot, hot tears of insult and abandonment streamed down her tender cheeks. She just couldn't understand how life could become so different, suddenly. All she felt was a growing resentment against the whole world. Till thirteen, she had not had a care. She had led the most happy-go-lucky days. Anything she had done had been agreeable. Everything she had said or done had been acceptable. Now, without warning she had fallen totally out of favour, as if she was no more the same person.

It was bad enough to have, what she had, every month. It was painful and uncomfortable to wear the thick pads Ma gave her, which she made with strips torn out of Thakuma's old dhotis and then rolled up with cotton wool. Sometimes, she even had to wash the strips and reuse them when Thakuma ran out of dhotis. She felt like vomiting, having to do that;

holding them under the tap, with the clotted blood flowing out into the drain; then, having to wash them with soap. She felt so unclean. She bathed and bathed and poured buckets of water to wash away any stains on the bathroom floor. Even then, she could smell the blood. Oh, how she hated, hated, hated being a girl!

The worst thing was when she began to be aware of the transformations occurring in her body. She felt self-conscious the way her dresses were growing tight around her chest, showing up the first, small bulges of her breasts. She spent hours in front of her mirror, trying to figure out a way to hide it. She was losing control over her old, familiar body and it made her acutely embarrassed, having to face the world. Gradually, Indira changed into a silent girl, introverted and sullen. She began to shun the company of people, preferring to stay in her room, or up in the terrace, among the potted plants of Thakuma's kitchen garden.

It was during this lonely stage of her life, on a full moon night that Indira had a disturbing experience. She lay on her bed, watching the pale glow of light through her window, making shifting patterns all over the walls, the floor and part of her bed. There was nothing particular in her mind but an acute awareness, as she listened to the rustling leaves of the guava tree outside her window. Suddenly, in her sensuous, half-conscious state, she saw a shadow move by her bedside. She felt its presence, like breathing upon her skin. She wasn't frightened of the shadow—it seemed familiar. But she was afraid to let the shadow know that she was awake. Instinctively, she stiffened, holding her breath and squeezing her eyes shut, till they hurt. After an interminable moment of suspense, she felt something stealthily press up like fingers between the fleshes of her thighs. The feeling was so painful and strange, that she could have screamed. Yet, for a moment, she wanted to feel it more, as if it would lead to some kind of pleasure. Then, a fear took over and tightening her legs together, she rolled away to the other side of the bed.

There was a slight squeak of the door, as the shadow escaped. Indira opened her eyes and realised her bed was soaking wet with her own perspiration. Yet, she was shivering with cold. Could it have been a nightmare? Trembling, she covered herself with the handmade quilt kept at the foot of her bed. But for a long, long time into the night she couldn't sleep. She could still feel the shadow breathe on her skin and the feeling between her legs kept coming back.

She thought of Ma, probably deep asleep now, after an exhausting day, Thạkuma must be asleep fitfully, in the other room but couldn't have heard her door squeaking from so far away. However, one thing was certain in Indira's mind. She could never, ever, talk about this occurrence to them, with no one, to be precise.

It was way past midnight before she sank into sleep—dreaming of being in a strange room, alone with him. She was sitting on his lap but was struggling to get down. He held her with one hand, while the other was trying to grope up her thighs, under her dress. It would be a long struggle, beyond the early hours of the morning, till she was too exhausted to struggle.

The Wish

All the devotees had left by late evening. Many had come from as far as the 24 Parganas and they couldn't afford to miss the last train. Shiva Ratri was one of the most festive religious occasions celebrated by the Ganguly family, with more than a hundred devotees coming to their home, on their own initiative, not wanting to miss the grand 'Bhog Prasad'. The grand preparation was done in their spacious terrace. Large mud ovens for cooking the bhog, normally brought out on such festive occasions, were lined up at one corner of the terrace. A quarter of the terrace was roofed with tarpaulin and was set up to feed the guests.

Amalasundari fasted the whole day, along with her female relatives. Even little girls fasted, though they did it just for fun. The evening ritual of pouring 'Gangajal' on Lord Shiva's Linga, a phallic symbol in black stone, and then making a 'wish' was their favourite part.

As the night sets in, the excitement of wish-making peps up everyone. The unmarried girls prayed for a husband like Lord

Shiva, married women prayed for children, pregnant women wished for a male heir and widows wished for the welfare of their families. On Shiva Ratri, Lord Shiva was said to grant all their wishes. Amalasundari's Shiva had earned the reputation of being *jagrata*—the living God. The devotees had developed a lot of faith in her Shiva after witnessing miraculous events in their own lives.

Amalasundari herself was revered by many. Especially since the day she had been guided in a dream to find Goddess Chandi, under the roots of the banyan tree, in her garden. In the centre of her sprawling puja room was a jhoola, or a hanging seat, which held a strange, russet stone, resting majestically on a red velvet cushion, trimmed with gold tassels. Everyone swore that it resembled Goddess Chandi's face, with gentle curves at exactly the right places. With the help of a goldsmith, the face had been fitted with large, flaring eyes, a gold nose ring was attached to the mound that resembled a nose, and lips had been drawn with kumkum. A rich devotee had even crowned the stone with a jewel-studded tiara. Scores of people now came to make their pilgrimage to the Ganguly house everyday.

Ten year old Milli, Amalasundari's only granddaughter, had missed her school for Dida's Shiva Ratri. Her father was totally against it but didn't want to hurt his mother-in-law's religious sentiments. His wife used to remind him often about how her mother's spiritual powers had worked in their favour. So, Milli was there, with all her cousins, pretending to be fasting along with all the elders. It didn't matter that they had been made to drink milk in the morning and fed fruits in the afternoon. Their mothers conspired and made them believe that all this was part of the *Uposh*, or, 'fasting-diet'. What Milli loved was being a part of the whole enterprise—the stirring of the *khichri* in those huge iron kadais, the smell of smoke from the mud ovens, the mass-scale chopping of vegetable and fruit, the endless chatter and laughter of the women, their saris tucked in at their waists, their faces gleaming with sweat. She just loved Shiva Ratri .

Finally, the time for pouring Gangajal on Shiva Linga came; it was believed that by doing so we were bathing Lord Shiva. Milli briefly closed her eyes and poured the brownish water from the brass container. Actually she was supposed to pray for good exam results, but her heart said, 'Dear Lord Shiva, bring Tommy back to us.' She missed her gentle dog - Tommy, who ran around the garden, mad with ecstasy whenever they visited. He jumped on their backs and climbed up their bodies to lick their faces lovingly. Oh, Milli loved Tommy so much. She couldn't comprehend why he had gone away to Sodepur, as Bishuda, their servant had told her.

When it came for Amalasundari's turn to pour Gangajal, she was surprised that the first thing that ran into her mind when she closed her eyes was that Tommy hadn't eaten the whole day. She was about to call out to Bishu to ask him when she remembered that Tommy was in Sodepur. She was surprised and shocked that instead of making a wish for her family, she was thinking of Tommy. She prayed to Lord Shiva for His forgiveness for sending Tommy away, His most devoted bhakta during Shiva Ratri. Tommy was different from other dogs. He always spent his time guarding the puja room, it seemed he too was standing there in reverence of Lord Shiva. He was a strict vegetarian, which was so unusual for a dog, that he earned the nickname—'the Brahmin Dog' for himself.

Around midnight, the exhausted women gathered in Amalasundari's room. Tonight, the night of Shiva Ratri, no one was supposed to sleep. It had some religious significance. They spread out rugs, sheets and whatever they could lay their hands on and prepared to keep vigil together. It was going to be difficult but they thought that they would definitely try. The children leaped over the prostrate bodies of the women, chasing each other and laughing. This was after all one of those rare nights, when the early-to-bed rule did not apply.

After a while, Milli got tired of prancing around and lay down beside her grandmother.

'Dida, why has Tommy gone?"

In the lull of the moment, her question hung in the air like a bruise. Instantly in that silence, everyone was reminded of the gentle dog and missed him. Tommy had been a part of this family since the day Bishu carried him home from the pavement. He had no collar and had the most forlorn eyes one could ever imagine. He was a mixed breed and had definitely been abandoned. But the moment he entered, it seemed he had known their family for ages. Yes, Tommy was meant to be in our family.

Gradually, he was tagged as the clown of the household. He was so genial by nature, that he wagged his tail at anything that moved, he did not have the slightest inclination to bark, let alone bite anyone. After Tommy came into our family, our house was robbed and each time the thieves had managed to seduce him with pieces of 'neri' biscuit, the hard, cheap stuff, dogs are given to chew on.

'What a waste!' Bishu said later, 'They could have just given him a pat on his head and he would have become their life-long accomplice.' Jokes apart, Tommy was respected for his spiritual inclinations and there was one place he would never have allowed the thieves to enter, the Puja Room, where Amalasundari stored most of her family jewels, though no one knew about it.

'Yes, where *is* Tommy?' Everyone asked in unison.

It was as if they had suddenly realised that something had been amiss all day.

'He's gone to live in the Sodepur house for a few months,' Amalasundari said, in a guilty voice.

'The Sodepur house!'

'Shiben wanted to borrow Tommy because they're having a spate of robberies in their area.' Amalasundari laughed.

'To chase them or to invite them for dinner?' someone joked.

'Poor Tommy,' they sympathised, 'He missed Shiva Ratri.'

Milli rolled over onto her grandmother's abdomen. She loved to lie that way because Dida would then stroke her back gently, something that made her fall asleep in peace. From the heaviness of Milli's body on her stomach, Dida realised that Milli had fallen asleep. Gently, cradling her she deposited her little body beside her.

'Your daughter has gone to sleep,' she whispered to Milli's mother.

'I'm amazed she could hold on so long,' she replied.

As time passed, Amalasundari could hear the sounds of regular breathing,, 'Everybody has slept,' she thought to herself. She was still wide awake, thinking of Tommy in Sodepur. 'I deprived a Brahmin of his prasad,' she regretted. If only Shiben had not asked for him. Shiben was her nephew, and had come all the way to ask her this favour. The only other option that he had was to buy a dog and train him, which was an expensive and time-consuming procedure. Shiben's family was not so well-off so she encouraged their family to live in Sodepur house, which was lying empty. More than the compassion for her nephew, it was Amalaundari's fear of letting the house remain empty, which had made her take this decision. It was risky to leave one's home empty as the cases of *jabardakhal* was heard of so often nowadays. Amalasundari thought that by letting them stay there, she was doing them a favour unto herself rather than to them. It would save them rent and her suburban property would be protected.

Suddenly there was a commotion at the eastern side of the house, followed by Bishu's loud calling. She got up hurriedly and threaded her way through the sea of sleeping bodies.

'Thieves, or what?' she shouted out to Bishu, trying to arrange her disarrayed dhoti.

'What? Who?'

Soon everyone woke up on hearing the din. The sounds of doors being unlocked and Bishu calling out Tommy's name was followed by a deep, resonant bark of acknowledgement from somewhere far away, near the garden gate.

'Tommy!'

'It's Tommy!'

'Jaya Lord Shiva! It's Tommy!'

'I knew, Tommy couldn't miss his Shiva Ratri Prasad!'

It was as if from his subconscious presence in everyone's mind, he had suddenly sprung into the realm of reality.

Tommy was in bad shape. Bishu said that while he was sleeping in his room, he heard a painful howl from over the garage. The moment he called out his name from the window,

Tommy threw up his body on the cast iron gate, full length and started yelping painfully.

Even long after Tommy's return, Amalasundari's devotees came to see Tommy. They sat on the floor, beside him and petted him affectionately and clucked their tongues in wonder, careful not to touch his bandaged paws.

'Another miracle of Lord Shiva,' they said, nodding their heads.

No one could ever solve the mystery of Tommy's return. How could he have covered hundreds of miles? How had he known the way? Especially when he was taken to Sodepur house, he was carried on top of a truck full of furniture that had been covered by a tarpaulin, as it was raining heavily that day. There was no way Tommy could have been guided by any scent. His paws were raw and bleeding, which gave us a clue that he had followed the railway track. And that needed some kind of intelligent thinking on his part, something dogs without pedigrees are never credited for. He mustn't have eaten well for two whole days, while he was making the journey. And that emphasised not only his determination but also his perseverance.

Later Shiben had come to inform them that Tommy went missing two days before Shiva Ratri. He also told them that he had been depressed and had refused food ever since he had taken him to Sodepur. When everyone was sleeping he somehow managed to break the leash and escaped.

Though technically nothing made sense, Amalasundari and Milli had no doubts about Tommy's homecoming, about who had brought him here. It had to be the wish they had made.

The Dighi of Garh Chandipur

As the Founder and Principal of Pragna Niketan, Maya Purokayastha had to deal with some of the toughest situations in the school. She was respected as much for her dream, as for her grim determination that had seen her through. Pragna Niketan was no ordinary school. It was an institution that had defied gravity in the way it had come up and flourished. A donated house by a philanthropist, teachers who had left high and stable salaries so as to get involved in this social mission, parents who had risked their children's safe passage into successful careers so that they could become better human beings, Pragna Niketan was a daring and defiant statement against the commercialisation of education.

So, Mayadi, as she was known to her acquaintances, had the right to say what she said to Shubhojit Sen's father that morning. He had come to see off his fifteen-year-old son on a school expedition to a historical village site, some six hours' drive from Calcutta.

'Mayadi, can you ask the teachers to be extra vigilant about him? Can you ask them not to let him go swimming?'

Maybe it was the pressure of seeing off thirty kids and six teachers so early in the morning and having to arrange and revise class schedules and other details, Mayadi lost her famous patience.

'Mr Sen,' she said irritably, 'I think it's time parents like you stop being so protective about their children. Let them grow up and be responsible for themselves.'

She relented a bit, seeing the discomfiture on the gentleman's face.

'Six senior teachers are accompanying them,' she said assuringly. 'There is no cause for worry. They'll be safe.'

Mr Sen didn't press the matter any further. He knew Mayadi well and trusted her. He took the chiding in good spirit because he knew it was justified. They had often discussed these issues during their parent-teachers' meetings and he was well aware of the school's policy of encouraging self-sufficiency in every student. However, he would have been heartened to know that Mayadi had already given specific instructions to all the six teachers about not allowing certain activities, among them, swimming in any village pond.

Even then, the whole day after the children had left, Mayadi kept thinking about Mr Sen's request.

It was almost lunchtime when the two school buses entered Garh Chandipur's main road, a non-surfaced track, wide enough for two bullock carts to pass abreast. It was a prosperous village that was at one time under the aegis of a famous Gauda Kingdom. The remnants of a beautiful terracotta Chandi temple, built during those times, gave the village its name—Chandipur. This village also had remnants of the fort constructed during those times which still drew many tourists to this rural area.

They were supposed to stay in the local school building, in its two large classrooms, which the authorities had furnished with some beds. Amarda, the History teacher had come to the village a few days ago and had made all the arrangements. As a result of their visit, this village school was to remain closed for two days. Now, as the buses entered the large playfield in front of the building, thirty students, both boys and girls eagerly waited to jump out and explore the place. Most of them had never visited a village. They may have flashed past the countryside in cars and trains, but had no idea about how people actually lived there. This was part of Mayadi's effort to make her students more sensitive towards their soil and its keepers.

The moment the kids disembarked, they saw a curious crowd that had gathered at a discreet distance, watching them as if they were film stars, who had come for a shooting. The news of their arrival must have spread, because within seconds, the principal of the school, a bespectacled, middle-aged man, pushed through hurriedly and approached Amarda, whom he had met before. He greeted them and escorted them to their quarters. Then he left to organise their lunch, which soon arrived in brass pails. The brass thalis had been borrowed from the local zamindar's collection. The ravenous kids lapped up the food, which had been cooked by the same brahmin who cooked bhog during Durga Puja in zamindar's palace. It was a simple fare—rice, from the granary, daal, a seasonal vegetable and deliciously cooked fresh Rahu from the pond. It had the same aroma of puja bhog, simply because everything had been cooked in in fired mud utensils, the same way food was cooked for puja.

The main event of the expedition, a guided tour of the temple and fort ruins had been fixed for the next day. As there was no electricity, there would be no travelling by night. However, till sunset, they could explore as much of the surroundings as possible.

By late afternoon, the students had been divided into small groups, with two teachers leading each group, and they set out for the 'Palace', some half an hour's walk away from the school building.

The palace was largely in ruins. Situated close to a huge *dighi*, it had a fairly intact Nat Mandir; an inner courtyard surrounded by pillared columns and covered balconies. The Andar Mahal, though also in ruins, had been partially restored, and one could only explore it to a certain point, beyond which it had been walled in, to allow the present descendants of the zamindar family to live in privacy. All the outhouses were occupied by homeless refugees whom the landlord allowed to stay without rent but in lieu of service to the landlord in some form or the other.

The tourists from Calcutta soon found out that evening fell much more rapidly in villages, than in the city. And being the middle of December, darkness came earlier, anyway. The chill in the air forced them to clutch their sweaters and shawls closer to their shivering bodies. They stood briefly on the bank of the dighi, not able to spot the other side. It was so huge. The waters looked impenetrable, with hundreds of years of darkness trapped beneath it. They returned quickly to the school building, as the oil lamps and hurricane lanterns began to twinkle and glow in the dark, shutterless windows, occasionally covered by pieces of cotton *gamchhas* and torn pieces of clothing. In the twilight, the dark monumental structure of the palace looked monstrous and foreboding.

It was dinner time. Tired by the long bus journey and enveloped in silence, they ate hurriedly, eager to dive under the rugs they had carried with them from Calcutta. The boys retired into one room accompanied by male teachers and the girls into the other accompanied by female teachers. The doors were locked after brief goodnights.

'Shubhojit is absolutely mad!' Urmilla, Shubhojit's girlfriend whispered to her friends who were nestled in a single quilt. A muffled giggle and a 'sh-sh-sh!' roused the curiosity of Monikadi, the youngest and the friendliest of all teachers.

'What did I hear about Shubhojit?' she asked, approaching the bed on which ten girls huddled together under the rippling quilt, which they tugged at continuously whenever a toe or an elbow was exposed.

Very reluctantly, Urmilla pushed down the quilt from the top of her head, revealing just her forehead and eyes. Her friends twittered from underneath. Any mention of Shubhojit brought on a spate of teasing, ever since the two had shown interest in each other. Officially, affairs were discouraged in Pragna Niketan, though Mayadi knew it was unavoidable in a co-educational school. So, as long as there were no overt demonstrations on their part, such affairs were ignored. But Monikadi knew that something was on between the two, both of whom were in her class.

Urmilla was an intelligent and outspoken girl. So her interest in Shubhojit wasn't girlish and she probably would not have been interested in him had he not been bright like her. But there was one subject which he was not so good at, and that was English, Monikadi's subject. The whole thing started when she asked Urmilla, her star pupil, to help Shubhojit with his English. Ever since then, she had noticed how desperately Shubhojit was trying to improve in the subject. A couple of times Urmilla had stayed back after classes to help him out with the projects.

'Mad?' Monikadi's eyebrows arched up in mock surprise, 'Who?'

With this a peal of laughter shot up from under the rugs. This woke up the other teachers who were just dozing off. The reserve maintained between the students and teachers inside the school had relaxed somewhat, during the long bus journey. In the close proximity of the last few hours, they had shared not only time and space, but also their needs. In the course a certain bonding and shedding of rigid rules had occurred between Monikadi and her students, though, it had come easily and naturally.

To Monikadi's amusement, Urmilla forgot the cold and sat up, exposing various parts of tightly curled-up torsos around her, drawing loud protests and much desperate tugging at the quilt.

'Di, he says, he's the ancestor of the zamindar and that the palace belongs to him!'

'Really?' Monlikadi asked her, peering into her wide eyes. It intrigued her that Shubhojit had such an imaginative streak in him.

Meanwhile, all the heads had popped out from under the quilt.

'He's been going on and on about it,' they complained. 'He told the boys in Calcutta that he would take them on a tour of his palace.'

The other two teachers had been listening intently.

'How did he know that there is a palace here?' Moynadi, the senior-most teacher in the group asked.

'He just knew,' Urmilla replied.

'Maybe Amarda had told him about it, after visiting here,' Kajoldi, the Botany teacher suggested.

'No, Kajoldi,' Urmilla doggedly insisted, 'He knew from before.'

'Oh, there has to be some explanation,' Monikadi said impatiently.

This brought on a spate of arguments.

'He described the palace to its minutest detail, before coming here!' chorused Urmilla's friends.

'While we were touring the place, he showed us every stone, every brick, every curve!' Urmilla said enthusiastically.

Monikadi interrupted again, 'I'm sure he has visited this place before. That's why he knows the details of the palace.'

'No, Monikadi, he's never ever come to Garh Chandipur before. He swore it!' Urmilla said passionately, while the other girls nodded.

Monika tried to reason again, 'There has to be some explanation. I'm sure he's making all this up to scare you.'

'He would never lie to me,' Urmilla said with such great conviction that even the girls did not laugh.

Suddenly, in the silence, the hurricane lamp flickered, though the air was totally static in the windowless room. Then there was a commotion outside. Everyone jumped out of the covers and rushed towards the door. Moynadi held them back, opened the door just a crack and yelled into the cold night air outside, 'Ke?'

A beam from a torch jumped out of the darkness and Amarda materialised from somewhere, shivering in his pyjamas. 'It's all right now,' he said. 'I had to go and get some of the boys. They had sneaked out.'

'Sneaked out! In this darkness!' Moynadi asked indignantly.

'To the palace,' Amarda replied. 'Madcaps!' he added.

A sharp intake of breaths from the girls prompted Moynadi to shoo them away.

'Off to bed. Off to bed. It's an early day tomorrow,' she reminded them.

'What's this curiosity about the palace, Amarda?' Monikadi whispered through the door.

'I don't know. Some sort of story Shubhojit has made up about being an ancestor of the zamindar in his past life. The other boys are very taken by the story.'

'Madcaps!' he said again, shifting from foot to foot to keep himself warm.

'What scares me Amar, is that there's this Dighi nearby,' Moynadi said worriedly.

'No, no, don't worry,' Amarda said in an assuring voice, 'I won't allow them to go anywhere near it.'

'Tomorrow morning I'll take up this nonsense once and for all.' Moynadi mumbled and shivered as she locked the door.

In one corner of the temple ruins near Garh Chandipur, Shubhojit let Urmilla on to a secret. He told her that all his friends were wearing their bathing trunks under their shorts.

Shubhojit said in an excited tone, 'We just have to convince Amarda and Moynadi somehow, on our way back. If they say yes, then other teachers would not create a problem. We'll just have enough time to take a dip in my ancestral dighi, before we start our journey back.'

'You are just kidding yourselves,' Urmilla replied. 'They will never ever allow you to go swimming.'

'What's the matter with you,' Shubhojit pouted, 'I thought you were my best friend!'

Urmilla thought with a serious expression on her face and said, 'It's *because* I'm your best friend that I don't want you to go swimming—you idiot. It's dangerous . . . and . . . and . . . I'm scared that something might happen to you.'

'Nothing will happen to me, you silly girl. I won't drown—I'm a champion swimmer, or have you forgotten!' Shubhojit said in a proud tone.

'Moreover,' he added teasingly, 'How could I leave you and go away?'

Urmilla remained silent and sullen.

'What, don't you have confidence in me?' Shubhojit quipped and bent down. Without any warning, he wrapped his arms around Urmilla's knees and pulled her up, lifting her up in the air.

'See how strong I am! See how strong I am!' he shouted, wheeling her round and round, as Urmilla kicked and flailed.

'Let me go! Let me go!' she screamed in mock panic.

'Only if you convince Monikadi to let us go swimming,' he said, holding onto her legs.

'Shubhojit, please, she won't listen to me . . . okay, okay, I'll try . . .' she finally relented, because she didn't want others to discover her in Shubhojit's arms.

Exactly how and when the boys succeeded in wearing down the resistance of the teachers, and extracting the vital 'OK, exactly for fifteen minutes,' nobody knows. The teachers themselves do not know clearly about it now. The entire journey back from the temple site to the village school building had been extraordinary, to say the least. The trip which lasted about an hour and a half can be best described as the mental coup of kids over their teachers. Senior teachers, like Moynadi and Samarda, not known for being very extroverted, or even very friendly, let down their hair and sang '*Purano Shei Diner Kotha*' with them. Impertinent questions like 'When are you getting married, Moynadi?' were asked and answered without any qualms. And somewhere in-between all the joie de vivre they agreed to let the boys have a dip in the palace dighi, 'Just for fifteen minutes,' before they started their journey back to Calcutta.

The bags remained packed and ready in the schoolrooms, where the drivers of the school buses stayed back to keep an eye on them. But the three o'clock start for Calcutta never came. Around two o'clock, Shubhojit, following his classmates, descended the steps of the dighi into its greenish water. He slapped some water onto himself, to condition his body, as the six teachers and girls looked on from the banks, his feet slipped on the moss-covered steps.

'Bah-bah,' teased Urmilla, 'The champion slips before he swims!'

The other girls laughed. The teachers smiled but watched intently, wary about letting any of the boys stray out of their vision.

Shubhojit pushed into the water, and then glided out towards the other boys. Suddenly, his head went under the water, as if to take a dip. One, two, three, four, five, six, seven, eight, nine, ten. . . .

After some tense moments, cries emanated from the banks of Dighi,

'Shubhojit!'

'Shubho, this is not funny!'

'Shubhojit, come up immediately!'

'Oh my God, he's not coming up!'

Amarda, without saying a word, took his shirt off and dived into the dighi.

Nineteen, twenty, twenty-one, twenty-two. . . .

Amarda surfaced and let out his breath. He shook his head conveying that he hadn't found him. Then he dived again.

One minute, two minutes, three minutes. . . .

Sumonda took off his shirt and dived in. The other teachers crowded the edge of the water, shouting to the rest of the boys to get out of the water. Bibekda rushed off to the school house to get the drivers and the local authorities. The girls instinctively hugged Urmilla who had begun to weep and wring her hands.

Four minutes. Five. Six. Seven. Eight. Nine. Ten. . . .

Amarda surfaced, shivering and blue from exhaustion.

'I've spotted him. . . . He's lying there. . . . right at the bottom . . .' he said, making a great effort to catch his breath. 'I . . . I just can't keep my breath till that depth.' His voice broke in despair.

Forty-five minutes later, the body of Shubhojit Sen, fifteen-year-old son of Sumanto Sen was retrieved from the bottom of Garh Chandipur's dighi and was laid on its bank. The village doctor tried resuscitating him, but in vain. He was pronounced dead at five minutes to three. Urmilla was dazed at this sight and fainted. Monikadi and the girls carried her back to the school building

Once again the whole village gathered around in silence. Someone brought a white sheet to cover the body. . . . The sun went down on the other side of dighi, waning into a small reddish dot of light that lingered like a malicious smile.

Out of the shadows of the palace, a vision came streaking towards them. A wrinkled old woman with gray hair flying around her face and her white sari half trailing behind her gnarled body, she was like a spirit that had materialised out of the ruins.

'*Rakkhusi*!' she screamed. 'So you have devoured again How many more will you swallow?' The cry she let out was so primeval, that it sent a shiver down their spines. She ran madly towards the waters but a few men who had run out following her, managed to catch hold of her before she jumped.

Moynadi, who sat beside the body, waiting for the transport to arrive to take them to the nearest hospital, heard the villagers whisper how fifty years ago, this woman was the beautiful young wife of the zamindar and how she had lost her sanity after her eldest son was drowned in the same dighi.

Glossary

Aashirbaad	–	Blessings
Adhunik	–	Modern, contemporary.
Akashbani Kolkata	–	All India Radio, Calcutta.
Amavashya	–	The darkest phase of the moon.
Amish	–	Non-vegetarian food.
Amriti	–	Sweets made with urad daal paste in floral shapes, fried and coated in sugar syrup.
Aroti	–	A ritual act of worship in which a worshipper circles a lighted lamp around the deity, accompanied by ringing of bells, blowing of conch shells and beating of drums.
Baap	–	Father
Bakarkhani	–	A thin, crisp bread baked with white flour and *mawa*.
Balushai	–	A sweet made from fried dough and coated in thick syrup.
Bapi	–	A common Bengali nickname for father.
Basmati	–	A high quality fragrant Indian rice.

Batasha	–	A small, button-sized, crisp, rounded candy, made with sugar or jaggery, traditionally offered to deities after puja.
Beta	–	'Son', in colloquial Hindi.
Bhakta	–	Devotee
Bhatiyali	–	A particular genre of songs sung by boatmen of Bangladesh.
Bhog Prasad	–	Cooked food offered to the gods.
Bhondo	–	Fake person; one who cheats people into believing he is someone else.
Bishu'r Ma	–	Bishu's mother.
Bonti	–	Used by Bengali cooks before the use of knives came in. A fixture with a flat wooden base, with an upright iron chopper fixed on it.
Boroma	–	Literally, 'Eldest Mother'. A term of respect usually reserved for father's eldest brother's wife.
Bou	–	Bride / wife.
Boubhaat	–	A Bengali ritual held a day after marriage, when the new bride serves food to her husband's relatives.
Boudi	–	A nickname for sister-in-law (brother's wife).
Brahmin	–	The highest caste of the Hindus; the priest class.
Chamcham	–	A diamond shaped sweet.
Chandi	–	A Hindu goddess. One of the forms of Durga.

Chhod da	–	A nickname for the youngest of the elder brothers.
Dada	–	Elder brother.
Dadu	–	Nickname for grandfather.
Dakshina	–	Money given to priests after they perform puja.
Danis	–	Containers
De	–	Give
Dekchi	–	A high, round utensil, used mainly to boil food.
Desh	–	One's ancestral village.
Dhakai Parota	–	A rich, stuffed paratha with mincemeat and fried with eggs.
Dhora	–	Light it.
Dida	–	A nickname for grandmother.
Didi	–	Short form '-di', used as suffix with proper names, to signify 'elder sister'.
Digha	–	A coastal town of Bengal, popular for its beaches.
Dighi	–	A huge pond.
Doi Machh	–	Fish, usually carp, cooked in yoghurt.
Galda Prawns	–	A large species of sweet-water prawns.
Gamchha	–	Light handloom towels.
Gandharaj	–	A species of fragrant lime, native to Bengal.
Gangajal	–	Water from the river Ganges, considered sacred by Hindus.

Garad Punjabi	–	Cream-coloured ethnic silk from Bengal. Kurtas made from this hand-woven silk is often worn on festive occasions.
Garam masala	–	A combination of spices, consisting of cardamoms, cinnamons and cloves.
Ghadas	–	Metal pitchers.
Ghee	–	Clarified butter.
Gojas	–	A sweet snack made with rolled-out maida, fried in ghee and coated in sugar syrup.
Gotra	–	The lineage or clan assigned to Hindus at birth.
Gulabjaam	–	A reddish brown sweet made from balls of cottage cheese, fried in clarified butter and put in rosewater-flavoured syrup.
Haringhata	–	Famous dairy owned by the West Bengal government, was at one time the sole suppliers of milk in the city of Calcutta.
Hemonto Chattopadhyay	–	A famous Bengali singer.
Hilsa	–	A variety of fish popular in Bengal.
Hisheb	–	Estimate
Hookas	–	Smoking apparatus with an urn of water and a long pipe .
INA	–	The Indian National Army, formed by the Bengali patriot Subhash Chandra Bose, to fight for India's independence from British rule.
Jabardakhal	–	Forced occupation of property.

Jagrata	–	Living God.
Jamaai	–	Bridegroom
Jamadaar	–	Sweepers
Jaya	–	Victory
Jhoola	–	A hanging seat.
Kadai	–	The Indian wok.
Kaliyug	–	According to Hindu scriptures, Kaliyug or the Kali era is the last and the most sinful age of creation.
Kalshi	–	Pitcher
Kanchkolar chop •	–	Raw mangoes, boiled, and then made into chops.
Kapalik	–	A Tantrik, or worshipper of Kali in the tantrik philosophy.
Kasba	–	Name of an area in South Calcutta.
Ke	–	'Who?'
Khichdi	–	A congee made from rice and daal.
Kurta	–	The loose Indian shirt, worn over a dhoti or a pyjama.
Langcha	–	Sweets made with sweetened cottage cheese, khoa and flours of different cereals.
Lau	–	Gourd ('lauki' in Hindi).
Linga	–	The phallic symbol representing the Hindu god Shiva.
Luchis	–	Bengali puris made of maida.
Lungi	–	An ankle-length piece of cloth, stitched like a straight skirt and worn knotted at the waist.

Machhher jhol	–	Fish cooked in a watery gravy.
Majhis	–	Boatmen
Mangal ghat	–	The pitcher with a red swastika drawn on it and a stem of mango tree with five leaves placed in it, usually surrounded by rangoli, placed near the puja area.
Maramari	–	Fighting
Mashima	–	Aunty (A common term of respect for married ladies, for unrelated people).
Maya	–	Illusion
Meshomashai	–	Maternal aunt's husband.
Mistries	–	Workmen
Mocambo	–	An old and prestigious restaurant of Park Street in Calcutta.
Muri	–	Puffed rice.
Murti	–	Idol
Mushurir daal	–	Lentils (masoor daal In Hindi).
Nagras	–	Rajasthani hand-stitched *jootis* or pointed-toe shoes.
Narkoler chirey	–	Coconut chips made in the shape of split rice and boiled in sugar.
Naroos	–	A sweet snack made from coconut and jaggery, cooked together and rolled into balls.
Nayantara	–	White, delicate flowers, used as offerings to gods.
Neri Biscuit	–	Hard, unbranded dog biscuits.

Oh, Mago!	–	A Bengali expression resembling 'Oh , dear God!'
Paan	–	Betel leaf.
Padmar Ilish	–	Hilsa from the famous Padma river of Bangladesh, valued for its taste, as against hilsa from other rivers.
Pantua	–	Gulaabjamun
Parshey	–	A silvery river fish of Bengal.
Peda	–	A sweet made from sugar and evaporated milk.
Phodon	–	Tempering of whole masalas in oil or ghee.
Pishimoni	–	A term of affection for father's sister.
Pithes	–	A kind of sweet snack made with rice flour or ordinary flour, which is made into batter, fried in the shape of pancakes and stuffed with various kinds of fillings.
Pranaam	–	Obeisance, touching a person's feet to show respect or, joining one's palms, while bowing one's head.
Prasad	–	The food that is offered to the deity and then shared by the devotees as god's blessing.
Puchkawallas	–	Puchka sellers.
Puja	–	Worship (plural refers to the Bengali festival in autumn, when Goddess Durga is worshipped for four days).
Rahu	–	A species of carp common in Bengal.
Rakkhusi	–	She-demon who devours everything.

Rasbadas	–	Gramdal-balls stuffed and immersed in sugar syrup.
Rasogolla	–	A famous Bengali sweet made from balls of cottage cheese, boiled in syrup.
Rather Mela	–	A mela that is traditionally held on occasion of the famous chariot festival of Lord Jãgannath.
Salt Lake	–	A planned satellite township of Calcutta
Samaadhi	–	The trance-like state in deep meditation.
Sandhya	–	Evening
Saraas	–	Mud utensils, shaped like plates.
Shaheb	–	A man of European descent; a white man.
Shankhachud snake	–	A kind of snake with the design of a conch shell on its head.
Shashurbari	–	Father-in-law's house.
Shehnai	–	A musical instrument played in weddings to reflect the mood of the occasion.
Shola	–	Sponge-wood plant or cork tree.
Shondhikhon	–	Twilight, when night and day meet.
Shonir dasha	–	The bad influence of the planet Saturn.
Shukto	–	A mixed vegetable Bengali dish with a slight bitter taste.
Sondesh	–	A dry sweet made with cottage cheese.
Tangail	–	Famous cotton saris named after the place they are made in.
Tatwa	–	Bride's trousseau and other gifts exchanged between the two families, including fish

		and sweets that are displayed artistically for guests to see.
Thakuma	–	Paternal grandmother.
Thakurpo	–	Colloquial reference by sister-in-law for younger brother-in-law.
Thankuni patar rosh	–	Juice of thankuni leaves; very pungent and having therapeutic uses (Indian Pennywort).
Tui	–	'You' (Hindi 'tu').
Tuk-tak	–	Witchcraft
Uposh	–	Fasting
USIS Reading Room	–	United States Information Service , which runs a number of libraries and reading rooms in Calcutta.
Vadi	–	Little balls of soaked and ground lentil, sun-dried and then added to vegetables for flavour.